EVA ROZIER

Botox Is My Prozac

Mind Rejuvenation /
Where Science and
Spirituality Collide

BALBOA.
PRESS

A DIVISION OF HAY HOUSE

Balboa Press books may be ordered through booksellers or by contacting:

Balboa Press
A Division of Hay House
1663 Liberty Drive
Bloomington, IN 47403
www.balboapress.com
1 (877) 407-4847

Because of the dynamic nature of the Internet, any web addresses or links contained in this book may have changed since publication and may no longer be valid. The views expressed in this work are solely those of the author and do not necessarily reflect the views of the publisher, and the publisher hereby disclaims any responsibility for them.

The author of this book does not dispense medical advice or prescribe the use of any technique as a form of treatment for physical, emotional, or medical problems without the advice of a physician, either directly or indirectly. The intent of the author is only to offer information of a general nature to help you in your quest for emotional and spiritual well-being. In the event you use any of the information in this book for yourself, which is your constitutional right, the author and the publisher assume no responsibility for your actions.

Any people depicted in stock imagery provided by Getty Images are models, and such images are being used for illustrative purposes only. Certain stock imagery © Getty Images.

Scripture taken from the King James Version of the Bible. Scripture taken from the New King James Version. Copyright 1979, 1980, 1982 by Thomas Nelson, inc. Used by permission. All rights reserved.

Print information available on the last page.

ISBN: 978-1-9822-0024-4 (sc)
ISBN: 978-1-9822-0026-8 (hc)
ISBN: 978-1-9822-0025-1 (e)

Library of Congress Control Number: 2018903121

Balboa Press rev. date: 03/12/2018

Contents

Part 1 Follow Your Bliss: What makes you happy?

The Aging Process 1

History of Botox 3

History of Prozac 4

Brain Chemistry Affects..4

Letting Go of the Past..6

Smile..7

Power in Creating 8

Staying Conscious of Your Own Thoughts 9

Feel Good... 11

What You Focus About, You Bring About 14

Plant Some Seeds 16

What Do You Believe? 18

You Are Special... 19

Wake Up! And Become Aware 21

Source/God 25

Black and White: Make it Simple 27

When You Focus on Bad You Get More of It............................28

When Your Happiness Comes From Something Outside
Yourself.. 30

Ask, Trust, Allow 32

Allowing 34

We Are Not Taught To Think This Way.....................................36

Imagination Is Key 37

Write It Down 39

Simple Formula 41

What Is Stopping You 42

Who Are Your Stars?..43

Shift Your Paradigm.. 44

Reprogram Your Subconscious Side..45

How You Put Energy Out Into The Atmosphere 46

Use The Information You Have Gathered...................................48

Abracadabra! But it's Not Magic! 49

Wellbeing, Human Being, Just Being 50
Depression Comes From Not Understanding.....................51
Anxiety is Suppression 52
Disease Turns into Decay..53
Go From Understanding To Being Emotional About it- Faith....... 54
Chose Fear Over Faith? 55
Creation Over Disintegration 56
Will You Overcome Depression? 57
Problems Are Opportunities 59
Repetition Creates Your Paradigm 61
Anybody Could Have Anything They Want..........................62
Your Three Wishes 63
Draw Closer To What You Want By Your Thoughts...................64

Part 2 Operating Being Conscious: Are you on automatic thinking mode?

Change Your Life By Waking Up An Hour Early..........................65
Use the 5 Second Rule...66
Trust The Process 67
Trust It..68
Giving V/S Receiving..70
Guide Your Thoughts...72
Instead of Digging Down, Rise Up......................................73
What Is a Pain Body? 74
How Your Pain Body Manifest Itself Inside You 76
We Are From A Place Of Love 77
Send Love To The People That Have Hurt You In The Past 79
What Do You Really Want? 80
The Power In Writing It Down...81
Be On The Outside Of What You Idealize On The Inside 82
How Is Your Attitude Effecting Your Results? 83
Negative Thoughts v/s Positive Thoughts.............................83
How Dedicated Are You? 84
Is Your Life Worth It? 85
Signs And How They Are Guiding You 86
Your Spirit Guides...87
Angles Guarding Us 88
It Is What It Is..89

Part 3 Making Decisions: How is personal power put into action?

Going From Point A to Point B...91
Find Your Earthly Destiny 93
Perceive & Achieve..94
Choose Your Purpose and Attain It 96
It Does Not Matter Where You Are Now..96
The Power Of Guiding Your Mind Into Direction...............................97
Success Begins With A Clear Picture in Your Mind's Eye 101
Clarity Can Be Achieved...103
Being A Leader..105
Guilt and Negative Emotions 106
The Ego- How It Effects Decisions...107
How Happiness Is A Decision 108
Are You Ready To Have Understanding 110
Failure is NOT Reality..113
There Are Spiritual Forces Within Yourself................................113
The Gift of Speaking It...115
Food For The Soul...116
Declutter Your Energy Field...116

Part 4 Happiness, Health & Wealth: What does the bill to yourself say?

What Do You Owe Yourself? 119
Is Your World FLAT? 120
Stepping Off The Cliff And Flying 122
Flying v/s Failure- A State Of Mind 123
Recognize Fear and Freedom 124
The Universe Is Always Expanding 125
Communication with Vibrations and Frequencies of Thoughts...126
What Do You Tell Yourself? 128
Disease and Being At Ease 130
Our Bodies Are Made of Flesh 130
Write Your Price Tag, Your Value, Your Belief 132
Treat Yourself and Others How YOU Want TO Be Treated 134
How Do You Relate To Others?..135
Are You Lucky? Say It! and Then It Is 136
Principles of Science and the Laws of The Universe 137

Part 5 The Success Principle, Going the Extra Mile: Are you at a turning point?

Quality, Quantity, Mental Attitude 139

What Do You Accept? 140

Want A Better Circumstance? 140

Want to be Compensated For Your Services? 143

Excel In Your Line Of Work 143

Contrast and How it Plays Into Success.....................................144

Be Original..145

Imagination To Gain Advancement..146

Be Self- Reliant..146

Master Procrastination..146

What is Your Purpose? Your Intent?..147

Become in Alignment With Others 148

Use Nature to Help With The Force Needed- Mother Nature's Habits 149

Part 1
Follow Your Bliss:
What makes you happy?

The Aging Process

*"As I grow older, I pay less attention to what men say.
I just watch what they do."- Andrew Carnegie*

Our self-image is key in defining our outer appearance. As we age we have loose skin that sags, spots that start to appear somehow overnight, eyelids that droop, crow's-feet that stare back at us in the mirror, lines that form across our forehead and not to mention what goes on with the inside of our bodies. It is a law of this universe, the law of aging. We cannot help the fact that as our years on this planet increase, our age increases and we start to look old.

Yes, you heard me right, the law of aging. We live by laws in this world don't we? What is a law exactly? A law is a phenomenon of nature that has been proven to occur whenever certain conditions exist or are met. A law effects every human being in the same way not matter what race you are, what ethnicity you are or where you are on this planet. Now, this law of aging is pretty self-explanatory. There is no special formula that is needed to express that yes, we get old.

Is getting old just physical though? Is our physical body effected by our subconscious mind? Yes, yes indeed it is. It is also determined by many other factors as we all know. Rather than focusing on what is given though, our thoughts about our own self-image can affect the rate at which the aging process occurs.

Do you feel old? Are there days that you feel like you look older? Have you ever noticed how feeling old makes you also feel sad? Do aging and depression go hand and hand, are they married? Maybe? If so then how do we stop feeling old? We start with something outside of ourselves, our thoughts.

Researchers are finding out that our mental patterns could be harming our telomeres- the end portions of our cell's DNA, our genetic make-up. Strange but true, our thoughts are affecting our lives and our health as a human being. Studies have shown that people that are cynical, hostile and pessimistic people have DNA strands with shorter telomeres on them. These people have an increased aging rate, an increased rate of heart conditions and age related illnesses. What is even more interesting is studies have shown that those people than hold on to their past also effected the telomeres in a harmful way. Rumination, the act of rehashing problems over and over only makes us feel bad. When we feel bad, we age and we get sick.

Nobel Prize awarded winning **Elizabeth Blackburn** that found the key to slowing our aging process said "We have control over the way we age all the way down to into our cells."

Do what makes you feel good instead. It's so easy yet so many of us are programmed into subconscious thought patters that create our world in which we live in every day. My world is different than your world and your world is different than mine. This is because perception is reality. My reality is totally different than yours. We all give contrast to this plant Earth. We all live our lives in deep levels of thought and our thought are the most powerful ammunition we have. We have control over how we feel, we have control to direct our thoughts into a feeling of clarity, abundance, happiness, fulfillment, purpose and all other positive aspects of feeling good. Follow me throughout this book to get some Botox for your mind. Clear out those subconscious wrinkles that are aging you. Come with me for some brain power rejuvenation.

<u>History of Botox</u>
General Information Here

Botox used for wrinkle reduction started by accident. In 1987 Dr.'s Jean and Alastair Carruthers' started peri-orbital wrinkle reduction experiment. In 1989 FDA approved under the trade name of Botox (onabotuinumtoxin A) to be used for strabismus and blepharospasms. So, initially botulinum toxin "A" was used for various eye problems including blepharospasms (involuntary blinking of eyes). By accident patients started to notice that their wrinkles went away when they got the injections. In 1989 physicians expand the use of Botox for off labels uses. They started to return to their ophthalmologist to get more of it not because of the spasms of the eyes but because they wanted it, it made them look better. When we look better, we feel better. When we look better, we are more confident, we are more social and we are more outgoing. Also, looking in the mirror is not as painful, we start to gain our self-esteem back. It took up until 2002 for FDA to approve the glabellar region (between the eyes) of the face to be used as a cosmetic wrinkle reduction medication. In 2013 FDA approved it for the crow's-feet region and in 2017 approved for horizontal forehead lines. Keep in mind that even though these areas were only just approved as "on label" uses for cosmetic Botox, they were used in these regions as "off label" uses all along.

The FDA should approve Botox injections for treatment of depression. Okay, that's funny but why not? *(Any licensed physician can legally prescribe any FDA approved medication in any way that may benefit the patient.)* The premise stated here may seem a bit out there, I know. It's true though. We hold physical image so high in our society. As we age we lose our identity and then it becomes a downward spiral from there.

History of Prozac
More General Information

Ironic but true that in 1987 Prozac was approved for treatment of depression. It was the most prescribed medication in 1988 in the U.S. market! It was the first product in a major class of drugs for depression called selective serotonin reuptake inhibitors. Prozac works by increasing the brain reuptake levels of serotonin (the feel good chemical), a neurotransmitter.

Serotonin effects several aspects in our bodies mainly being the mood that we are in. Because of all the hoopla around these SSRI's there have been multiple studies on the effects of serotonin and the affects it has on us. What is boils down to, when we eat better, we have a positive mental attitude, we exercise, we are social, we have a routine and when we have constancy in our lives, serotonin is at a higher natural level.

Although serotonin remains a mystery still to scientist and will not allow full knowledge of its effect on the brain and body. The brain is a difficult organ to study in detail. There is so much we as human beings cannot explain.

Brain Chemistry Affects
A pinecone shaped gland?

So much affects our brain chemical state. From our environment to the way we express religion, it is all proven to affect the chemical makeup of the brain. This is not a research paper and I am not a scientist. Most of us out there living our daily lives have so much going on all around us not even realizing the profound affect that our decisions we make have on the way the chemicals are released and how they are stored in our brains and bodies.

As it was stated above, scientist have only scratched the surface of understanding our brain. It is definably understandable knowing that our brain is just simply hard to experiment on. How are we supposed to pry into a human beings mind to see what happens on a daily bases? Anything is possible and the research taken place in the past has proven that we have more brain power than we can ever even imagine.

Can you influence the world around you with the power of your mind? A leading Russian scientist and a professor of computer science and biophysics, states "With our consciousness we can directly influence our world." There is an unseen world of energy and of the most of influential people in our world have a deep inner knowing of this fact. Bioelectric photography is used to prove this about our bodies.

The pineal gland is said to be "the third eye" in our brain. This gland is located deep in our brain and is responsible for creating pictures in our brain. It produces serotonin and melatonin, the same neurotransmitters that are said to be responsible for our happiness. Melatonin regulates sleep cycles and when our sleep cycles are off in the body our bodies have a sublet but significant reaction to the lack of a regular sleep pattern. DMT is another molecule that is said to be released from this gland which is Dimethyltryptamine. DMT is sometimes called "the God molecule". Various studies have linked the lack of a circadian rhythm to having migraines, depression, increased blood pressures or increased water retention and so on. The pineal gland is said to be in a hardened state in some of us due to fluoride intake in our water supplies. Do your research on it. Our government requires fluoride in our water to reduce cavities but third world country citizens smile with amazing white teeth. The pineal gland plays a crucial role in regulating our body's psychological wellbeing and it may hold the key in unlocking the true potential to all of humanity.

In this pineal gland there is floating water with crystals that have piezoelectric properties. Long word, right? Mainly this means that there are particles that reflect light. There is also another thing called piezo-luminescence which is from a crystal being compressed that create photons which make the light you see. There is another property called piezochromism which describes the tendency of certain materials to change color with the application of pressure. When DMT is the main chemical that seems to do this big burst of colored light. These little crystals are floating around in our brain!

There are photo receptors on the pineal gland people! PROVED, STUDIED, DISECTED. Our brains have a third eye in the middle of our brain!!! Ok, how did they know this a long long time ago? Does fluoride turn the lights off? Something to think about and to learn about. If you have not looked this information up at this point, you should.

Letting Go of the Past

Say this to yourself, "Letting go is not hard to do". When we tell ourselves something on a regular bases, we must honor it. Looking forward, moving forward, heading straight ahead is something we as human beings must learn to do in order to eradicate depression for our world. Simple and easy to do once you have the knowledge on how to do it. What are you holding on to? Does your identity stem from your past hurt and pain? The people that have hurt you in your past have unconsciously done so, they should not hold the blame for your present day.

Jesus said "Forgive them for they know not what they do". If Jesus was living now he would probably agree that they were living unconsciously not knowing, living that automatic life, and acting without the subconscious mind having any say so.

Forgiveness is giving up the hope or the idea or the wish that the past could be any different or changed. Although, many of us think forgiveness means just accepting what has happened to you in the past. Indeed forgiveness is accepting that is HAS happened to you, not accepting that it was alright that it happened but accepting that is HAS happened and now ......and NOW......what is it that I can do about it? Forgiving, your past, quit wishing that it was any different. Just let it go so your past does not hold you a prisoner.

Practice this thought that letting go of past circumstances gives us freedom to create a new and better future. Your future is more important than your past. Your NOW is more important than your past. Doing this will take you to the next level of being the best you that you can be. Release it from inside your body, do not hold grudges.

Your past does not define who you are, it should not be a part of your identity. Who you decide to become NOW defines your identity and where you are going in life.

It is proven that holding on to our past effects our complexion, the wrinkles you have on your face, your youthful glow that is lost, weight gain and on and on and on. Holding on to the past ages us, it effects our bodies down to every cell. Simple effortless being, living your life now, just being in the now gives us an amazing power.

Eckhart Tolle said "Realize deeply that the present moment is all you ever have."

Let go, let it come, let the world happen. You will not lose who you are by letting go of your past. Direct your thoughts into this present moment. Listen to the birds when you walk outside more. The birds are created for us to learn to be present. Embrace what is, praise what is, be grateful for what is now and then more will come. Most of us are never fully in the present moment because we are unconsciously in the belief that the next moment is more important than this moment. Then, with in a blink of an eye, our whole life has been missed, which is not NOW.

Smile

There is a hidden power in smiling. Some years ago I found myself pressured to force a smile on my face when deep down I was not happy. The situation was not perfect, I wanted to be something else, do something else and it made me sad inside. Then, I noticed I wasn't smiling. Such a simple act to do is to smile but it came so hard and unnatural to me at one point in life. Then, I discovered when I smiled daily and made a habit of it, the simple act of smiling took me into a more positive state of being. I actually forced myself to get into the habit of smiling more often. Now, I am actually addicted to it.

Smiling has been studied and it has been proven that those who smile more often live longer! Even if you are forcing yourself to smile, your body doesn't know this so the chemicals released in our brains is the same. We start to feel better the more we smile! Studies have shown that the neurotransmitters serotonin and norepinephrine that when we smile or laugh we experience a boost in these feel good chemicals. Smiling and laughing are married as well. Find yourself smiling more and then you will find yourself laughing more and it is contagious! Yes, laughing and smiling is contagious!

It doesn't cost a penny to smile! It's easy! Just wear a smile with those nice jeans you wear, wear a smile with your favorite shoes, and wear a smile to compliment your brand new sunglasses. Wear that smile to your next interview! There have been many scientific studies involving smiling. We exude confidence when we smile. Dental hygiene is so important. If you have dentist phobia, face that fear knowing if you don't you won't live as long. Smile and live a long happy life.

Power in Creating

We are in a constant state of which we expect something from someone. We want someone else to love us. We want to put the blame on someone else.....for all the problems we have in life. We are all looking for the feeling of happiness, the feeling of joy, the feeling of abundance, the feeling of completeness, the feeling of having connections and the feeling of happiness in the external forces. This is where we need to actually need to take a journey inward. Emotions such as fear, passion, joy, grief, love, hate, peace, courage, contentment, uneasiness, disgust, clarity and hurt all come from somewhere within us, somewhere deep inside. Why do some people struggle so much? Those that are lacking inner peace, inner joy, and inner love. Let's learn how to find this within us so then we can give back to the world. Ask the universe how may I serve you?

A dear friend of mine said in her understanding of this concept "It's like the world wants to make us focus on the wrong things instead of the inner born things." This statement is so simple it's true.

Creating is not about competitiveness. Creating takes the act of visualization. We all, every single one of us is creative in our own way. We each have different finger prints for a reason. If it's a book you want to write, visualize it finished first. If it's a store you want to open, visualize the store move in ready first and focus on it until you've created it. If it's a painting you want to paint, visualize it completed first and then the actual piece of art will move through you until that feeling is complete. There is so much about our world that does not promote creativity. It's almost like you are looked at as "gifted" if you can plug into a source and create. The truth is we all have the same exact ability with practice and focus. Not only is that but self-discipline key.

Discipline is not a pleasant word but the act is much needed if you ever want your visualization to manifest in life. Making a decision, self-discipline and visualization all equal your goal or creation. If you want to learn, grow and transform in life, taking a spiritual journey is so important. How to create this spiritual journey? First learn to become free of fears. Then ask yourself who you want to be in the world. Then have a vision of your journey. Small changes make big changes. You may think making a certain decision is a small thing but decisions or choices actually make our world.

A great minded man named **Napoleon Hill** stated "Discipline comes through self-control. This means that you must control all negative qualities. Before you can control conditions, you must first control yourself. Self-mastery is the hardest job you will ever tackle. If you do not conquer self, you will be conquered by self."

Staying Conscious of Your Own Thoughts
How do we learn how to not be an excessive thinker?

Ideas make you do, not be. Human being is meant to learn how to just be. What it boils down to is we are basically eventually pushed into **just being** at some point during our life time. As we age, our bodies give out, we depend on others, and our senses fade is when we are forced to just be. Have you ever been in

9

the nursing home and watched that 90 year old woman in the wheelchair that is blind and lost her hearing. **She is just being**. She was forced to do so from the aging process that some of us go through. How will this help us learn to live a more balanced life you may ask? Learning to just be is something that most of us never learn until it's somehow forced upon us. During the state of just being our minds are in a different state, we become more aware of our surroundings and tuned into the higher power of our universe.

Worry about tomorrow, worry about yesterday, worry about the last sentence you just said or the next sentence that's about to be said rather than just being in the moment........

How do we stop self-talk in our head? Is thinking an addiction? Is thinking a pseudo sense of self? To let go of thinking may feel like the letting go of eating for some people. **Thinking can confuse you**, thinking can actually be the **culprit of down fall in life**. The over activity in the mind is a coping skill we unconsciously have a habit of rather than being responsible for the present moment. Having our presents is lost because we are having excessive thoughts. Not thinking about our thoughts or being conscious of them.

Practice conscious thinking by going outside and perceive your moment without giving a name to it. Say you see a bird fly by or a snail on the ground, perceive it without thinking you see a snail or bird. This should be underlying, you shouldn't think about not thinking either. Just go outside and be. Just breathe in and breathe out. Our minds want to wonder and when a thought comes watch the thought but do not follow the thought just watch the thought then just be again. This teaching from a well-known spiritual advisor is such a simple concept to grasp but we do not practice this enough and without practice it is hard to do. Meditation is the same concept, this is meditation. It has been proven that meditation is eye opening for all of us if we learn how to and take the time to.

You have a choice, be fully in the here and now or choose to drift off into thinking. The benefit that being in the now gives us is that being in the now moment releases the hold of anxiety and depression from our body. Depression is holding on to past ideas and anxiety is being anxious about the future. It all has to do with past and future. Sense the aliveness inside of you. Be still and know that thoughts can be directed. You do have the control of your thoughts. **You are the boss of your thoughts**. This has been said to be **the secret of life** when understood. When you have an inner transformation in consciousness happens.

So there is a physical body and then there is a psychological me. Perception is our reality. What we perceive as ourselves we are living today. This moment is always just now. Become free of compulsive thinking. Are you aware that your thoughts ramble on? When there is no awareness you are the self-talk, you are your thoughts. It's only when we are aware that our thoughts can be directed that you see how your thoughts can cause you to go in circles. You look at these thoughts and you quit to justify these thoughts. Guilt seems to rule the fact that you must be thinking about this and that. There is freedom when we withdraw from these thought process patterns. When we become aware of our thoughts, we are conscious of our thoughts then we are in the moment instead.

Feel Good
Allow your feelings to be your guide-

Most of us think once we have the brand new car we will feel good. Once I get my brand new house, I'll feel better? Once you meet your soul mate, you will feel better? But the truth is you have the power to feel good before you actually have any of those things. Go inside yourself and use your mind to make you feel good. The truth is you have a choice to be happy. Decide you are going to be happy and just feel the happiness. Once we have overcome resistance to being happy it is in then you are able to basically trick your mind into believing it has whatever it is you wanted already. Then once that is done, we start to attract the reality of that feeling to us through the change in our outer frequency.

Everything has a vibration, a frequency and with human beings it is our thoughts that create that vibrational frequency. It is **scientifically proven** that everything in this universe has energy attached to it. In the simple act of just feeling good we are able to raise our vibration and attract to us what matches our vibration. Let our bumble bees teach us this by understanding how they know which flower to go to for nectar. As they fly around buzzing on their venture for nectar, the bees are actually able to detect the electrical charge from that flower. Yes it is true and scientifically proven. Plants generally have a negative charge and send out a weak electrical signal. We now know that our bumble bees have a keen sensitivity to this electrical charge. Pretty cool huh? Most of us never stop to think about this but it proves that we all have an electrical charge.

There is a well-known law of the universe called The Law of Attraction. Just like The Law of Attraction there is another law called The Law of Vibration. **Bob Proctor**, one of our world's great mentors of life, states "The Law of Vibration accounts for the difference between mind and matter; between the physical and the nonphysical worlds." This law states that anything that exist in our universe, whether seen or unseen, broken down into and analyzed in its purest and most basic form, consist of pure energy or light which resonated and exist as a vibration frequency or pattern. It is so true that when we have good thoughts, we choose to have good thoughts, that by nature more good thoughts will follow. The state of being in vibrational harmony or alignment with others with thoughts the same as you, the same as your good thoughts will naturally accrue. Feeling good is a choice, choose to feel good no matter what your circumstance then you will bring into your world others that feel good as well. It is a cycle.

This is not only a Law of the universe, it is a principle taught from over 50,000 years ago from a book called the **Corpus Hermeticum**. In this book there are seven principles to our universe taught and one is the principle of vibration. This information is nothing new, it has been taught for years but so many of us just do not understand it.

Science revels that everything in the manifested universe is all together made up of pockets of energy, quantized units vibrating at specific frequencies. This may sound weird but quantum physicist have shown that while matter appears to be solid (**everything is matter**) when you look at it or perceive it but when you look at it through a high powered microscope it is true to see matter is broken down into the smallest of components. These components include: molecules, atoms, neutrons, electrons and quanta (the smallest particles that are measurable).

Most of what is perceived to be as **matter is mostly empty space interspersed with energy!** All of this is not talked about in regular conversations with others due to the lack of understanding behind it. **It is simple though**, everything that is of manifested material including **you and me** is comprised of energy and empty space. Solid forms of matter which is anything or everything that appears solid is the frequency of vibration of energy that makes it up. Our thoughts make up our energy. Simple enough to digest? Think about this for a minute while you are vibrating.

This is so important in our life to just hold onto for the rest of your life once it is learned. Knowing **this information should be where it ALL BEGINS for you.** As your conscious mind thinks thoughts of a certain quality, these thoughts become engraved deep into our subconscious mind. The thoughts then turn into the output of our dominate vibration. This vibration you have as your dominate state of thinking resonance with other similar vibrations and draws them into your life. There is a metaphysical law to understand as well, the whole entire universe as we know it is our mind. Everything around us is affected by our vibrational state, our environment, the animals near you, the people in your life, the inanimate objects, and also the 'empty' space is affected by your vibration and then reflects back to you.

How are you feeling at the present moment? Look at the people in your life, your best friends, your co-workers, your pets, your home, your clothes you wear but just everything, you've brought it into your universe. Your feeling NOW, how you feel in this present moment dictates your vibration. Just know that if you have positive feel good feelings you will get back from everything around you the same positive feel good feelings.

The great **Earl Nightingale** said "Learn to enjoy every minute of your life. BE HAPPY NOW. Don't wait for something outside yourself to make you happy in the future. Think how really precious is the time you have to spend, whether it's at work or with your family. Every minute should be enjoyed and savored."

<u>What You Focus About, You Bring About</u>

Energy flows where attention goes- this is nothing new either.

Have you ever bought a new car then after you bought it you noticed how many other cars are just like yours out there on the road? Or have you ever been thinking about a new pair of boots you want then notice everyone that has them on that you may cross paths with? This is the lesson. Are you telling yourself how broke you are? You will get more of being broke the more you think about being broke. Are you thinking about reaching a goal in life and do you think about it daily? Multiple times a day? Well if you do then that goal will be achieved just by the law of nature. This is the Law of Attraction, it is a real law that exist in under our universal laws. It applies to everyone that has a subconscious and conscious mind, it applies to all human beings no matter your sex, your race, where you are in life or the color of your hair.

Think about how amazing our world is really. God is the ultimate artist of our universe. God resides in us. God is love, love is an emotion, and our emotions affect our manifestations.

Einstein understood this and when he said "Imagination is more important than knowledge. For knowledge is limited, whereas **IMAGINATION** embraces the entire world, stimulating progress, giving birth to evolution."

How are you using your imagination? What are you thinking about? Be grateful for what you have today! Be in the now, stay present and focus on what it is you have now. What does your

14

imagination show you inside your mind? What is your perception? Do you need to change your reality? Because our perception is our reality, use your imagination to change your perception which in turn will change your reality. You have to practice this, exercise this, and visualize what you want for your life. Think about it daily, write it down and make a card that you leave in your pocket, look at it from time to time throughout the day. These dreams, your imagination can bring into your life what you've always wanted. What do you want? Just right now, stop at this point and write it down! Make a decision on what you want, visualize it in your mind's eye, activate your pineal gland, and then you will raise your frequency and then your awareness will expand and things will come into your life beyond what you can even perceive at this moment.

Simply put we become what we think about. Walk around today like you already have what it is you want. Feel the emotions attached to it, feel like you have your ultimate life style already. The more you practice this, the easier it gets. Our minds cannot decipher reality from the imagination at this point. This is another concept that has been scientifically proven by studying the minds of athletes. The greatest of teachers or mentors in life understood this and understand this concept with great importance. People like **Earl Nightingale, Oprah Winfrey, Dr. Wayne Dyer** and so many other infamous teachers understood this great way of using their imagination to manifest what it was they wanted for their life.

What is success? Who succeeds? The only man that does succeed is the man that has a steady realization of a worthy ideal. A goal? A vision? Work towards a vision with your imagination and let it continue to expand. The man that says "I'm going to do this" and then he does it. That is success.

Earl Nightingale wrote a book called "The Strangest Secret In The World" long before the book and movie made called "The Secret" existed. The Law of Attraction is not something new age or a new concept, it has been around for centuries! In this book he explains the same exact thing that the movie and book "The Secret" says. Basically he teaches that the key to success or the key to failure is the fact that we become what we think about. All of the great teachers, philosophers, and profits in the past disagree on various topics but if you do your research you will begin to see that this is one thing they all agree on.

Buddha said "All that we are is the result of what we have thought. The mind is everything. What we think we become."

Instead of competing, we only have to do one thing, we have to create. Our world is a competitive world but if you focus on the competitiveness then you will only get more of it. Instead create something for yourself. Our human mind is powerful, seeds or thoughts we plant in it will grow with more thoughts. Thoughts is the water for the seed of an idea or goal. Most of us are only operating on about 10% of our abilities. Use your mind, plant a seed with imagination, create a goal and work towards it by thinking about it. It's so simple that most adults cannot comprehend this lesson.

Jesus said "Go! Let it be done just as you believed it would." Matthew 8:13

Plant Some Seeds
"I planted the seed, Apollos watered it, but God has been making it grow"- 1 Corinthians 6:3

Now we are not talking about actual seeds here, we are only taking about an Idiom such as to lay the groundwork for something that can develop or expand in the future. In the natural world we actually do physically plant seeds to make them grow. We water them, give them sunlight, protect them from the cold, and add nutrients to the soil and so on. Those physical actions make the plant grow. What if you started to look an idea like that as well?

Plant an idea in your mind and with your thoughts make it grow. Our thoughts are like water. I cannot explain it to you in any other way other than letting you know the more you think about an idea after you've came up with the idea, the more that idea will actually physically manifest itself to you. Once you gain this understanding then your world will do a 360- no doubt. You begin to look at your reality in a completely different way. People start to walk into your world. If you understand this concept- BAM!!!! Watch your world grow.

Let that idea sink in, think about it, think about it again, and again and again until you understand this process. It's not really rocket science but seems to be as if there are people out there still not understanding this. I was talking with a friend last week about this topic. I was telling her about how ironic I thought it was that money was green. She had never put the two together either. I suggested our government did that on purpose to somehow subconsciously implant a seed as well. Although the conversation was quit eye opening to me, she did not quite understand it. Be open and do not close yourself off to this understanding. There are usually only a small percent of people that really understand how this works and I am defiantly still learning. Learning something new every day THANK YOU UNIVERSE.

Have you ever noticed that? Our government decided to make money green. Can you grow money? Exactly! How? By your thoughts. Do you have a green thumb? What do you tell yourself? Are you horrible with plants and keeping them alive? Do you take care of them enough tending to their needs? Give them enough water? Sunlight? Keep them from the cold? Or do you expect that some external force is making them grow? Physical plants will only lack from the lack of the physical action. When that physical action is done with love this is when they flourish.

Our thoughts are the water, your visualization is the sunlight. Mental growth is the same and the plant, just as anything that comes within yourself is. You can only keep it alive and growing with a mental and emotional state of being. Our universe is a very magical place.

How may I serve you?

What the late Dr. Wayne Dyer taught was something that was known well before his time. He learned these lessons along the way like we humans do and he figured it out. He taught to ask the Universe this question. How may I serve you? When we reach out and serve in we will find our purpose. This is an ancient concept and it's so relevant.

Put your attention on service and not paying attention to outcome. Plant the seeds in your mind that will help serve others.

When we live in meaning, we live in purpose. We should stop being so attached to what the outcome is and putt the attention on your serve instead. There is an energy that is taking care of everything. Something else is really in charge than all of us. God, source or whatever you may choose to call it. There is something larger than all of us.

Put your focus on severing someone else. To touch someone's life is more valuable than any money. How can I serve? How can I be gentle? How can I be reverent? Surrendering to the universal laws and to something that's bigger than you. You can run an entire business this way. We all want to be fulfilled. Before we leave this earth, we want to touch others' lives deeply in some way.

In the morning the messages being sent to us are about what you can and by what you can't do. The morning time comes and our days begin and automatically we are given a title. How does society define you? When the afternoon comes, after you've worked your shift, it's about connecting to an energy that is in everything that is surrounding you. Get back to nature and just surrender to what is bigger than you. The truth is we are only a thought away from being the person we want to be in life. Become aware that you are more than just your physical being. Plant a seed in your mind and watch it grow by your thoughts which will in turn control your emotions then in turn promote a certain vibration in the world. What you focus upon will start to show up in your life. Watch it all grow.

What Do You Believe?

Are you what other people think of you? Are you what you have?

Know that everything will always workout for you. Move away from feeling like your entitled, move away from being afraid. We all want more and more and more and more and no accomplishment is never enough. Instead give to others learning that you have more the more you give. Give your time to someone today. The earth never says to the sun "you owe me."

Water is soft. A rock is hard. What do you think is the stronger entity in a stream? The rock or the water. We all know it is the water. What does water do? Water helps plants grow. Water helps life to flourish. The softer we become, the more flexible, the more you accomplish we are. So many profits reference to water. Earlier we talked about thoughts being like water for our seeds we've planted to grow.

Tao verse 76: "The living are soft and supple; the dead are rigid and stiff. In life, plants are flexible and tender: in death, they are brittle and dry. Stiffness is thus a companion of death; flexibility a companion of life. An army that cannot yield, will not be defeated. A tree that cannot bend, will crack in the wind. The hard are stiff and will be broken. The soft and supple will prevail."

The Tao also teaches this by telling us that when we die we become rigid and stiff but at birth we are soft and flexible. Pretty amazing stuff to learn.

When we make a statement to our universe like "I'm not creative" or "I'm broke" then you believe that for yourself so it must only manifest itself to you. When you start believing and knowing you are the creator, you are creative, and that you have abundance instead of that you are broke. Instead have a deep knowing that you have it all inside of you and start telling it to the universe, say it out loud.

You Are Special

As children we believe most of what we are told. Santa Clause is real and the tooth fairy is real until we get old enough to figure out that, no they don't really exist. While we are small our minds seem to grab ahold of ideas and dreams at an exponential rate. Our dreams sore and our imagination is endless. We also are extremely influenced during those precious years. Somewhere along the way, our path in life as we age we lose this ability to really dream intensely.

My father use to tell me "You are special" and I believed it when he told me this as a small child. Every action I did as a child, I did knowing that I was specially made and offered something to the world that nobody else had exactly as I did. I knew God made me and that I came from a higher place than earth. I knew this without any doubts.

Joel Osteen has said "There is treasure on the inside, you have something to offer than no one else can, if you don't step into your destiny and release your gift, then this world will not be as bright as it should be."

If you're completely comfortable all the time then you are not using your faith. Faith is key in having expansion in your world. Step into the unknown, unexplored places knowing it will work out and it will. Sometimes we are offered an opportunity, we may be afraid to take the plunge but God would not have presented this offer to you unless he know that you have what it takes to make it work. Step out of your comfort zone knowing you will fly.

Our life is like a tiny piece of sand on the oceans shore. We are here for a split second then we are gone. We can spend our whole life to reach a goal then to only find out that is not what will complete you. The road may lead to a dead end full of stuff or the lack of stuff. But it is only when we think bigger then God starts to act bigger in our life. You are special and do have a destiny here on earth to serve others and to serve this universe. Something higher than you gave you an assignment and he equip you with exactly what you need for his plan on this earth.

Everyone has a light inside, we all are unique down to our fingerprints, down to our souls. We are not here by accident, we all came into this flesh into a reason. To experience life and to make a difference here in the world. Even in small ways when we make a difference it resonates into a big difference. We must change our mindset in life to allow Joy into our life. Hit the easy button! "That was easy".... Tell yourself that. I am telling myself that as I write this book.

Negative thoughts may creep in and corrode your mind. EXCUSES! Do not dwell on the negative thoughts. As those thoughts come to you then take a conscious look at them then disregard them. The more you think the negative thoughts, the more of your reality will be negative. The more you say to yourself, I cannot do this today because I feel sick or thinking it is going to be so hard and it will never work out then the more you will get back that in your life. Thank you universe that this will be easy, that this will not be a struggle, that this will flow easy to me, that the words will come to me, that my dreams and goals can be accomplished. Quit allowing those excuses rule your life. You take control and become conscious of your thoughts. Do not allow negative thoughts keep you from your victory. Don't let weariness in your world!

We are all special and unique. Be amazing, do what you were sent here to do. It is not our job to be like someone else. Quit idolizing people. Celebrate your uniqueness. Just to be able to touch one other person's life is more valuable than any outcome you may receive back. To give is to get. Know your purpose here on earth is solely to serve. We all poses a different skill set, use your skillset to give back to the universe and quit worrying about what you will get back from it. You are special inside and out, never quit believing this.

Wake Up! And Become Aware
Appreciate everything you have!

While we sleep our bodies get replenished with some much needed energy. Our cells are vibrating high and we feel refreshed with the correct amount of sleep. The first thing in the morning catch your first thought. Notice that your mind will go at a higher speed of thinking than it was before you slept. It is in this moment you must stop those flourish of thoughts coming and going. If you only were to let your first thought be "oh this bed is so soft" or "this pillow under my head feels so amazing" or "my body is at a perfect temperature" or "It feels amazing knowing I have another day to live." Saying positive affirmations to yourself, just appreciating things around you to yourself will open the day for a fresh start. Awaken to the power you have in your conscious state.

In reading this book you are opening your mind to a different way of thinking, a reprogramming of your sub-consciousness. When you open yourself to this reprogramming you also open yourself to being limitless. Do you desire and know your desires will be manifested now? How does that make you feel? For me, it took not being guilty for having more wealth than others. We are only responsible for our own manifestations in life though. Pay attention as you apply some of these lessons to your life. Pay attention to how it makes you feel to walk around knowing that you are able to draw close to you your dreams and desires.

Know that instead of choosing to have any negative emotions attached to your own success only have positive emotions attached to it.

Do this small becoming conscious exercise: nobody will know you are doing this.

- Consciously Smile
- Bring attention to your breathing
- Place your palm on your abdomen
- Breathe deep into your gut
- Exhale
- Breathe consciously
- Inhale: count 1,2,3
- Hold your breath : count 1,2,3
- Exhale : count 1,2,3,4,5,6

Do this for 6 more cycles

- At the end of these cycles consciously smile
- Say to yourself: I return to the moment 3 times

There are only two states of being. The stressful limited state of being or the unlimited not stressful state of being. Do you feel separated from the universe? Do you feel anxiety or depression? Do you feel disconnected? Do you feel conflicted? We must learn how to be drawn to the more beautiful state. We must learn to not have conflict and confusion in our life. We must learn to be in a state to feel joy and heartfelt connections. This limitless state will offer a state of having peace in your life. This state will give you actual inner state. A beautiful state is your foundation for your life. Life starts to feel beautiful when you are in this limitless state.

Are all you good at desiring? Do you desire? Do you take action? Take action! Quit only desiring. Daydream all day long about having what you feel will make you happy. Do not allow your only action be the daydream. Your action is required to manifest this daydream. Do not fall into the trap of feeling as if you will never get there. Have faith that your dream will manifest itself in your life. Have faith knowing that the action required to do so will come to you. Faith is the bridge between where you are now and where you are going. Do not stop and turn around on that bridge when you get half way. Know without any doubts that everything that is happening is the road leading you there. Turn your aspirations into reality.

Try doing this exercise when you can get into a place of aloneness: Feel yourself being in a state of connection.

- Sit upright with your spine extended
- Place your hands on your thighs with palms up
- Touch the tip of your thumb to the tip of your index finger
- Breathe slowly
- For the first breath keep your thumb and index finger together
- For the second breath move your thumb to your middle finger
- For the third breath move your thumb to your ring finger and so on…
- Do this for 8 complete breaths
- If you have wondering thoughts, keep touching the fingers
- Bring your attention back to the breath
- Then inhale deep and an your exhale making a humming sound like a bee
- Your hum must be strong enough to create a vibration in your head
- Do this for 8 cycles just like the previous step
- Bring attention to the point where inhalation begins and exhalation begins
- Count 1,2,3 between your inhale and exhale points
- Still moving your fingers along with each cycle of breath
- Do this for another 8 cycles
- At the end of that cycle
- Breath in count 1,2,3

- Still focusing on the finger tips
- Exhale and hum to yourself an affirmation like "Limitless" count 1,2,3,4,5,6
- Feel yourself expanding
- Imagine yourself dissolving into light
- Imagine you have no boundaries
- Feel that you are not separate from anything or anyone
- Feel a sense of fulfillment and joy

This lesson just taught above is a way to meditate. It is a way to connect with your inner state as well as everything around you. It is a way to connect with God, with source, with the higher power. It is a way to get into a higher vibration, a higher state of being, a limitless state of mind. This lesson must be practiced on a regular basis to stay in alignment with this state. There are other forms of meditation but the most ancient of prophets agree that in mediation we gain a higher sense of living. Through meditation our lives can begin to transform. Try doing this exercise one time a day for seven days in a row then analyze how you feel after that seventh day.

The late **Dr. Joseph Murphy** was an amazing author that understood so much about how this universe works. He states "Your desire in your prayer. Picture the fulfillment of your desire now and feel its reality and you will experience the joy of the answered." Now what he was saying is so true. To be able to hold a picture in your head is to imagine it but really hold it there. He is saying that when we use our imagination along with the spiritual faith we hold when we pray that our desires will come into manifestation. There is a process to this, it's not like you can just imagine a Mercedes Benz being parked in your drive way and it will appear. You have to do the work, you have to study the laws of the universe and basically know without any doubt that your desire will manifest.

Prayer is also a way to create a higher union with God. We must understand though we must say prayers than ask God how we may give to him instead of him giving to us. Say a prayer like this "Dear Father in heaven, Thank you for the wonderful skills and gifts you've so freely given to me. I surrender all I am to you.

Come guide my path as I look for new work. May I always serve you and others in the new adventures that await me." Instead of praying something like this "Dear Father, Give me my health back, I promise I will do better. Give my family abundance and keep my source of income flowing to me." As you can see there is a clear difference in the form of prayer here. Just keep in mind "How may I serve you." With every prayer you will learn to become conscious of what you align with God about. Getting into alignment and becoming in the limitless state of being in the goal.

There is a five step process taught for the prayer process as well:

- Relax- let go of worries, have faith that there is a higher being.
- Concentrate- Turn your thoughts inward to a place of peace and positivity
- Meditate- Feel the security in a higher being than you, to God, connect to everything
- Embrace the Silence- focus on the quietness inside, God waits here for you
- Give Thanks- Give affirmations of thanks in all ways to God

Appreciation and saying thank you make us conscious of our daily life. In this way we start to become aware and awake in the present world we live in today. We begin to turn away from our old habits and our old ways of thought in practicing these lessons.

Source/God
God is love, God is forever expanding, God is
the creator, and God is source energy

Until we realize and understand that there is a higher power in our world we cannot resonate to the high flying frequency that is needed to have true success in your life. Just by choosing to read this book, it is put into your awareness about something you may have not thought before. When you shake up your world with including God, God receives the new and improved version of you things begin to happen. The only reason you ever stand in negative emotion about anything is because you're still standing in LESS THAN the new and improved version of you. There is no regression in living a limitless life, there is only moving forward and expansion.

Know that who you are now is just that.
Who you will be is what is to come.

What is God? This is a question you may find yourself asking at some point or another. Energy. What is energy? I think therefore I am. An energy can neither be created nor destroyed only transferred from form to form. God is the energy that is in us, created us and is us basically. God is everywhere and nowhere at the same time. Like we breathe in air, it is unseen but we know it exist, so is God. God is inside us like air is in us. Our bodies take it in and it helps our atoms vibrate at a certain frequency. This topic is extremely political, wars happen over this topic but when the truth is Love is an energy source and if God is love than God is energy.

Have you ever noticed that the way our trees look and the way our blood vessels in our bodies look the same? Not only that, so does the alveoli in our lungs, all of our central nervous system, our lymph system resemble branches of trees. Also, leafs they look as if they have blood vessels running throughout their bodies. Lightning, look like tree branches. Who designed this? God. Fibonacci sequence is God's finger print. The way our bodies have been designed and the way our universe has been designed all have this number sequence inside them. Look at the pattern of sunflower seeds inside a sunflower. 55, 34, 21. Pinecones does the same number sequence. The way a wave crashes, petals on flower, our fingerprints, our eyeballs, a starfish, the nautilus shell, our bones, the spiral of the galaxies above us. This is not a "new age" moment like some may claim. It's a simple yet very complex understanding of who God is or what God is flows within us and outside of us.

Think about the beginning of time, years and years ago all of life started with a single atom which is formed of electrons, neutrons, protons and empty space. The empty space is filled with a high vibrating energy source. Have you ever wondered how it is amazing that the similarities in an atoms structure mimics our solar system? Just something to ponder on for a moment. Matter is made up of atoms, with all that empty space what does this mean? It means that everything has an electrical charge.

Black and White: Make it Simple

Feeling good is the path to wellbeing in life. Working harder isn't the key, it's simply feeling good. When we focus on feeling good, our perception of reality takes a hard shift in the right direction. So, when you start to practice the control you have over how to feel good you may start to notice your desires seem to be highlighted. You may start to start to daydream about your unborn child, your future spouse, your business that someday you hope to start and so on. You only desire these things in thinking that they will make you feel better, right? The thing is you may actually find yourself getting frustrated in the lack of having those things because it makes you feel like you are actually lacking that. Instead focus your attention on the moment.

Our world is full of color. We have succulent flowers full of a various range of colors. We have beautiful clear blue oceans that contrast with our blue sky so perfect. We have lime green VW buses. We have luxurious butterflies that are encoded with perfect proportions and colors that camouflage their environment. We have a world full of bright colors. It is important to not have your desires be full of colors though. You must think in very simple terms about how your desires will be great. Go black and white, make it simple.

Instead of thinking I want to have a baby one day, a wife or husband one day, a new business one day we should be thinking very simple thoughts. Simple ideas should pop in our head like I'm so looking forward to things falling into place, I'll know it when I see it, I'll know what to do when the time comes, I'm going to live happier ever after, I will be guided every step of the way. These ideas are simpler in drawing to you your manifestations desired in life. The key is having faith basically. All of the more simple ways of thinking about your future imply you know you will have it and look forward to it. You must know like you know like you know that these manifestations will come forth in your life. Focus on how it makes you feel when you tell yourself things like things are always working out for me.

Once you work your way towards having that manifestation actually present itself in your life is when you can start to add detail of color to it. Get very specific about knowing what it is you desire, make a decision, grow that idea with the thoughts about it, write it down in detail, then it will come to you.

When You Focus on Bad You Get More of It

Let's discuss The Law of Attraction for just a minute here. Some of you reading this book may have never heard of this law, others may know it well and some of you understand it perfectly. The Law of Attraction says that that which is like itself is drawn to itself. In other words what you are thinking about attracts other thoughts that are similar to it. This is why when you wake up on the wrong side of the bed, when you tell yourself that, it must be and you have things happen to you all morning long to prove this to yourself. Your keys get locked in your car, your coffee spills all over your lap, your hose get a huge rip just before you walk into the office, your boots come untied and you trip walking up the stairs. Things like that can happen to someone on the frequency of negativity.

There is power in our thoughts, if you turn your attention to your achy bones then your bones will ache more. Change the subject in your mind, think about how good strawberries taste when covered with chocolate. Don't hold on to that negative thought that floated across your mind. Recognize it, see it but do not follow it. Let it float on by. Let it go.

When we hold onto the unwanted in life then we stay in a vibration or frequency that keeps not allowing wellbeing in life. The attention to the lack of wellness does not make us sick, it is the attention we hold close to the lack of many different things. We should focus our intentions on the experience of physical

28

well-being instead of focusing more on the lack of it in our life. Deciding to turn your attention to the well-being experience will not only help us to recover from an illness more quickly, it also prevents illness and gives us wellbeing. So when you are sick instead of focusing your thoughts on how bad you feel, turn your thoughts towards something that actually makes you feel good. Lay outside in the sunshine, go for a walk in fresh air, meditate, do what it takes to make you laugh, laugh some more, read positive affirmations, create something and share it with a friend, do something for someone else no matter how small it is, ask the universe how you can serve it today.

"Give your attention to what makes you feel good, thereby releasing your attention for what makes you feel bad."- **Abraham Hicks**

There is a small tool you can use to help you become more conscious of what you are focusing on called a "Focus Wheel" in which Abraham Hicks teaches us on how to get into a state of alignment and positive flowing frequency. The steps include:

1. Draw a circle in the center of a sheet of paper
2. Write a statement such as "I want to have confidence"
3. Then out on the side of that circle draw a line and write on it something like: "It feels so good knowing I am a special creation apart of this universe."
4. Then draw another line from the circle and write on it something like: "It feels amazing to be an inspiration for others to achieve their dreams."
5. Then repeat this process over and over until your inner circle is full of statements branching off of it.

This will help you get into that positive state that allows your vibration to raise higher, you will attract more positive thoughts to yourself the more you practice this.

Eva Rozier

<u>When Your Happiness Comes From Something Outside Yourself</u>

We are programmed to believe we have to change what is going on outside ourselves. You give the power away to someone else, some type of outcome, or someone else. Literally we have been trained to rely upon to perceive reality through our senses such as seeing, hearing, smelling, tasting and touching. You may say to yourself "I need him because I love him" or tell yourself "my happiness depends on having a TV to watch every day". The truth is when you think those types of thoughts then you literally are calling that into existence. You are giving the power of how you feel to be controlled by something outside of who you are inside! Do not give this power away! There is a STRONG power we hold inside to have control over our own happiness regardless of any compensation or outcome. It is true that there are only 5 senses we are taught about in grade school and we are taught to live our life relying upon these senses. What we are not taught is to pay attention to what is going on inside ourselves. Perception, the will, memory, imagination, intuition – these other 5 senses are not taught to us.

- ❖ Do this right now: just once to yourself ....Say:
    - ❖ I am happy
    - ❖ I am healthy
    - ❖ I am wealthy
    - ❖ I am secure
    - ❖ I am worthy
    - ❖ I am positive
    - ❖ I am blessed
    - ❖ I am grateful
    - ❖ I am beautiful
    - ❖ I am confident
    - ❖ I am courageous
  - ❖ I am excited about today
    - ❖ I am loved

> Other than a little awkward, how did those thoughts
> make you feel? Say them to yourself with truth
> behind them. This is a small exercise you can do
> daily to gain a strong sense of a positive self-image.

Our thoughts go out into the universe, are accepted or agreed with and then are brought back to us and create the world around us. Most of us walk around thinking, thinking, thinking not even paying attention to our own thoughts, we are just doing it. Train yourself to look at your thoughts from a higher sense of self from inside yourself. Miracles will start to happen once you begin to understand this law of the universe, The Law of Thinking. Once you begin to understand this law is when your world starts to transverse into something magical. You have the control to change what goes on in your subconscious by consciously thinking instead of subconsciously thinking on autopilot. Learn how this works and miracles will happen in your life. Your subconscious mind will start reprogram itself.

Happiness is an emotion and you have control over this emotion. You can choose to pay attention to a funny movie and to not focus on the downfalls in life then your emotion starts to change. When our emotion changes our vibration changes and then we start to attract those with the same vibration as ours. I like to think that the universe hears everything I am thinking about. When I find a negative thought slip out, I visualize a vacuum sucking it back up as trash. I do not want the universe to get ahold of a negative thought ever!!! Because this is the truth. Your thoughts create your life. It's so simple but maybe not the easiest concept to accept.

Once you can accept this and understand it you will begin to be aware of how your thoughts are contributing to our life. Start being nice to yourself. Start to tell yourself you CAN do this instead of you CAN'T do it. Start holding a different self-image you have for yourself. See yourself as the person you'd want others to see you as and do it TODAY even if it has not happened yet. It does not matter where you are as far as having formal education or not having a formal education. What matters is where you are going. Start believing in yourself. Now, I know some levels of advancement require a certain degree to be attached to your name. BUT how this works is if you want it, are a match to it with your vibration then you will be it whatever that may be. If it requires you to further your education, believe you can do it and take the action required to do so. DO NOT WORRY ABOUT THE DETAILS, IT WILL ALWAYS WORK OUT. If it's a new business you want to start and you only have your GED, believe you will get there, hold an image in your mind, then you will without any doubt hold it in your hand one day. Because this is true, if you can see it in your mind indeed you will hold it in your hands.

Ask, Trust, Allow
Have faith….

Our universe is full of abundance. The oceans are full of endless sea creatures, our skies have endless amounts of birds flying high above us, there are endless amounts of fashionable clothes to wear, cars, jets, and money, and you name it. There is no ending in the amount of water that is on this planet. This universe has an abundant amount of stars in the heavens. There is no endless source of the amount of love that is available to us in this universe. Ask the universe for whatever your desires are and know like you know like you know like you know that you can attain it. Trusting, having faith and allowing this manifestation to materialize in your life is all the same thing but first you must ask.

Joel Osteen says "When you focus on being a blessing, God makes sure that you are always blessed in abundance." He also says "Act like you are blessed. Talk like you are blessed. Walk like you are blessed. Put actions behind your faith and one day you will see it become a reality."

Now Preacher Joel Osteen has the concept down pat. He speaks with clarity each time he holds church. He has powerful messages and is famous for his positive speaking abilities. What he does is touches us all by stimulation our positive emotions. He tells us that he believes in each and every one of us. He tells us that we are all full of treasure and that we are sent her as Godly beings to share love as one on this planet. Not only does he teach with great passion but he actually lives what he is teaching. Is there any question in your mind that he does not understand this concept of ask, trust, allow? It's having faith. This is no secret, it is has been taught throughout ancient times that having faith is important in having abundance in life.

We are a physical extension of God. There is a stream of external energy from outside ourselves that flows to us, in us and is us. Love is energy and God is love. Before we were even born, God existed and will continue to flow even once the physical being that you know experiences passing away. Every single living thing on this planet like plants, animals and humans all experience death, there is no exception. Spirit, which is who we really are, a ball of energy full of vibrational frequencies, is eternal. All death is, is a changing of the perspective of the eternal spirit. If you are standing in your physical body and connected to it then you are eternal in nature, you must never fear any endlessness. We are eternal consciousness.

Your emotions let us know how much energy you are attracting towards you in this moment by the wanting of the desire in your mind. Your emotions also know if they match your desire or match the absence of your desire. For example, a feeling of excitement and passion, your emotions show you have a very strong desire, also rage and revenge also shows a strong desire. If you're in a thought vibration thinking about what you want and feeling pleasure from the thought, then your vibrations are calling that towards you which is ALLOWING. If you are feeling revenge and blame when you think about your desire then you are aligning your vibration to have the very absence of what you desire.

Lear to pay attention to how you feel. Allow your emotions to be the indicators to choices you make in life. You're emotions do not create but they rather indicate. Follow your bliss is a positive thought, right? If following your bliss gives you anxiety then your bliss will not play out in your reality. Instead have a blissful state of being first then your desire will line up with you. There is something very special about learning how to not listening to all the chatter that goes on in the world. Be still and make the decision that you want to feel good and you want to feel good more than anything, so much that you're willing to not focus on the opinions that don't allow you to feel good, about everything.

Instead focus on going within and aligning with what it is that makes you feel good.

Dance in the rain, splash around in mud puddles, who cares if your neighbors think you're crazy? Did you feel good doing it? That's the point. See your surroundings as a hot buffet of thoughts floating all around you, take your pick about what you are thinking about. You choose. The less you think of having any problems the less you have any problems. Trust that it will be given to you and act like you already have it.

Allowing
Believe in yourself

Learning how to allow a desire come into my life was the hardest concept for me to grasp. Once I did, my world started a shift, my world started to flow with a more directed stream of thoughts. Instead of staying in my comfort zone, I stepped outside of it and took a big leap of faith. When I took that leap of faith is when I just trusted that something outside of me had my back or that I had wings and could fly. I knew any decision I made was neither right nor wrong but it didn't matter anyway. What mattered was the fact that I made that leap. No decision that has been made or choice that has been made is truly never wrong because failure is never truly ever failure. Failure is just that one thing in life that points you into the right direction. We all go through things that are only guiding us in the correct direction of our destiny. Our destiny has all to do with the images you hold in your mind, your imagination. This is allowing. When you ask the universe for something and take no action to call it into your life then the universe will say you are not allowing it to be.

We know that our minds have the capability of holding an infinite number of ideas. When we gain a greater understanding of that these ideas we hold in our minds form an image. These images we hold express our own ideas of self-image, self-growth or self-limitations. **Dr. Joseph Murphy,** a minister ordained in Divine Science and Religious Science, said "True source of wealth: Your subconscious mind is never short of ideas. There are within it an infinite number of ideas ready to flow into your conscious mind and appear as cash in your pocketbook in countless ways. This process will continue to go on in your mind regardless of whether the stock market goes up or down, or whether the pound sterling or dollar drops in value. Your wealth is never truly dependent on bonds, stocks, or money in the bank: these are really only symbols necessary and useful, of course, but only symbols." He goes on to state "The point I wish to emphasize is that if you convince your subconscious mind that wealth is yours, and that it is always circulating in your life, you will always and inevitably have it, regardless of the form it takes." Now think about this for just a minute. This concept of "The Law of Attraction" states the same exact thing and Dr. Joseph Murphy was on this earth from **1898-1981** long before the idea of "the secret" or "law of attraction" was pushed to the public.

The truth is some people were born knowing how to apply this to their lives. **Oprah Winfrey** explained once that she understood this long before she even knew she was doing it. She went on to tell a story about how she held the idea of being an actress in the movie "Purple Rain" long before she even expected that she would be cast on the movie. In fact she tells a story about how she went on a casting tryout for the part she wanted and thought she didn't get the part but still knew somehow she was meant for it. Then she got a call randomly from the movie producers telling her she got the part months after she tried out for it. Oprah said she had no clue that was what she was doing but she was doing that with so much in her life already.

There really are endless stories about true successful people that actually implement this concept into their life naturally without knowing. Somewhere in their programming, in their subconscious mind, they learned this along the way but for a large majority of us, we do not get it. The picture just doesn't come clear to until we long for the picture of life to come into focus. It may be a traumatic event, something eye-opening that shook your world up that made you say to yourself that the old way was not working anymore. Out with the old, in with the new. That's exactly what I did and I can tell you that I have allowed some amazing things in my life just from holding strong and firm to my faith.

We Are Not Taught To Think This Way
Old life – New life

A paradigm is basically a way at looking at something. This word comes up often in the scientific world and in the business world. For example a paradigm in a business could be a new approach to drawing in a different group of customers leading to an increase in profit. In the scientific world a paradigm shift would be like when everyone thought the world was flat and then it was proven that the world was round. There are many of these paradigm shift that occur within our education systems, our scientific communities, and in our business worlds. As a human being we also have a paradigm imbedded deep in our subconscious. This is where our actions stem from and where our manifestations start from. How we think, our perspective or set of ideas about reality and our life.

When I was in grade school my mother left, I was only 6 years old. She had some things in her head to sort out during that time. My mother gave up her three children to move on with her life in the way that suited her needs. She left behind a husband and three children. Sounds like a sad situation and it was but it only taught me to handle my world in a very unique way. It was funny for me going to my friend's house seeing that they depended on their mother to cook, clean, do their laundry and wake them up for school when we did that for ourselves. My dad worked full time after taking an early retirement from the US ARMY. No words can describe the love I have for my Dad because I know he had it hard. I was six years old, the baby of the siblings, my brother was eight and my sister was eleven. Needless to say, my Dad had his hands full with three children on his own and working as much as he could. It was not his fault but there were times that I felt my needs as far as an educational standpoint did not get met. I'm sure there are many of us that have similar situations. Single parents home, small child and not getting the homework done because your one parent had too much load themselves. My grades always reflected that. I was scatter brained but it was because I lost the only thing I knew for discipline in life, my mother. She was strict and Dad, not at all. I grew up believing that I was only a C' student

36

until I graduated high school and went straight into nursing school. I was dating a guy at eighteen years old and his mother told me I was smart all the time. I started to think that too! I graduated at twenty years old with my LPN degree at the top of my class with a 4.0 gpa. The one thing I did different was tell myself I was smart and believed it.

Bob Proctor said "School gave us valuable knowledge. However school never taught us how to alter our old PARADIGMS. Therefore we frequently do not do what we already know how to do!" Our IQ does not tell us anything unless we are able to change the way we look at our world. Unless we decide that we really CAN DO ANYTHING when we apply our imagination and faith. He also made the statement that "We're taught to trade, we're not taught to give." It's true think about how much money you trade for your goods, what about giving and not expecting anything in return. Giving is always always always receiving.

If you have a child in school today I am sure you understand the rigid demands it places on their creative souls. Some children are more expressive than others, some are meant to be artist, some are meant to be inventors and some are meant to be healers, every child is different but they are all expected to meet the same level of educational memorization and application. Children have to depend on someone outside of the educational system to help shift their paradigm, be that person for them. You will be amazed at what the words you tell small children will do for them later in their life, your thoughts become their thoughts and then their thoughts make their truth. Teach this to them.

Imagination Is Key
"Logic will get you from A to B. Imagination will take you EVERYWHERE"- A.E.

Launch your rocket of desire and imagine you can have anything you want in life by seeing it first in your mind. What you have now is not what is important, what is going to come is what is important. Affirmations such as saying to yourself "I will make it" do NOTHING unless you can SEE it in your mind FIRST. See yourself walking across the stage with your diploma in your hand, see yourself standing in your new office because you got that promotion you wanted, see yourself holding hands with your soulmate and if you can see it, it will become into reality. The reason is that our minds cannot tell if what we are visualizing is real or imaginary. You HAVE TO SEE IT!!!

God or Source, whichever you prefer, gives us all kind of different abilities that we are born with. He shapes us all unique to his purpose to our lives. We all are born with differences, different features like the color of our hair, the tone of our voice, the texture of our skin, some have freckles and others don't, some of us are born short and others born tall. BUT IMAGINE THIS, there is one similarity each and every human being shares the same, we all have the gift of imagination. Imagination is the foundation of creation. Can you imagine what God's imagination is like!

A huge POWER is in the ideas we hold deep in our minds eye, our pineal gland. Einstein's impact on all of humanity came from his imagination and Karl Benz created our first automobile from his mind. Think about how much impact a few ideas have made in this world. How big is your imagination? Have you ever came up with an invention? We are nothing but animals without our minds, we have the same organs as a pig does! The effect you have on others is the largest amount of currency you will ever receive. Touching others' lives even in a small way will bring to you more joy and happiness than any amount of money can ever bring alone.

Being accepted as the apart of the group can be being invisible in this universe. Dare to ask the universe for your dreams to come true, imagine big and know that you can get there! There is nothing bigger than your imagination in your life. Fear may be running your life, you may not have the guts to step into unknown territory but I am here to tell you that you can trust the universe will not let you down. How will you serve the world? Ask the universe how you can serve it. Dream up your life, write it down, and hold it in your mind. Visualize what you want for your future but appreciate and be grateful for where you are now because where you are now does not matter, it is where you are going.

Jim Carry tells a story about how he wrote himself a check for $10,000,000 and gave himself 5 years to do so. He said the piece of paper fell apart but he kept it in his wallet. He said by the end of the 5th year he made that $10,000,000 for the movie "Dumb and Dumber". He goes on to tell the story about how he did not even have his GED and then was cast on the show "In Living Color" and then that brought one thing to the next for his career. He just decided he needed to do what he needed to do and not what society told him he should be doing. He said he did not conform to the group, he defiantly stands out. **Jim Carry** says "I believe in putting a rocket of desire into the universe and you get it when you believe it, you get it when you believe you have it." Although we may not think of Mr. Jim Carry as a mentor for life, he really is and he is one great one at that. His mind set, his paradigm was programed to tell himself that he can fail at what he doesn't want and he should take a chance at what he does want.

Write It Down
An idea is just a DREAM until you write it down, then it's a goal

Then the Lord replied: "Write down the revelation and make it plain on tablets so that a herald may run with it."- Habakkuk 2:2 in the Bible. This quote was shown to me by God just now, a source outside of myself. As I write words seem to come to me and at this very moment this scripture presented itself. There is so much truth in that scripture. When you write your goals down, it only gives you a stronger emotion attached to the desire. When your emotion becomes so strong is when things start to move, you start telling people your desire with confidence that it will happen without any doubt at all. You start to spread the news of your greatness that is on its way, you get more driven and passionate about it. The right words come to you, the right choices come to you, the right opportunities present to you and the right people start to come in your life. Your world starts to look different, you may have a AH HAH moment when you look around at how much your life has changed.

All these dreams cannot happen at once though. We are not able to shift in a 90 degree turn over night, it is the law of the universe. For example when you want to lose weight have you ever lost 10lbs over night? No, it takes time to do so. You have to start changing your thought process about your own self-image, you have to learn to let things go and eat healthy to have an achieved weight loss goal. So, all of your desires will not happen overnight or at the same time. If they did, your mind would not be able to handle it. But I am here to tell you that the small changes are HUGE changes and once you start using your imagination and writing your desires down, your world will change, do not let it freak you out. Let it excite you instead!!! Start to play with it in small ways on the daily bases. Start to always desire the best parking space in the parking lot, start to say out loud positive affirmations for others, and they see the reaction you get.

Do this and see what changes it can make for your life:

- ❖ Hang a chalkboard up where you will look at it daily.
  - ❖ Write positive affirmations on it every week.
    - ❖ Make a goal card to keep in your pocket.
    - ❖ Divide the year up into quarters for your goals to be met each quarter.
  - ❖ Look at your goal card throughout the day every day.
  - ❖ Read this book every day if it helps you think positive.
    - ❖ Get inspired by others accomplishments.
    - ❖ Cut the T.V. time down to almost nothing.
  - ❖ Get a journal and write your brain storms down.
    - ❖ Tell others about your plans.
  - ❖ Do not care what they think of you- you care about that.
    - ❖ WRITE YOUR IDEAS DOWN

Taking action on having your desires manifest in your life does mean that you have to actually do the work to have what you want. You cannot just expect that your imagination will bring to your life anything without actually writing it down and taking action. You have a dream, you can live it.

Simple Formula
$$E=mc^2$$

What does $E=mc^2$ mean? Well most of us know that this formula is from Albert Einstein theory of Relativity but what does that actually mean? Relativity is just a method for people to agree on what they see if one of them is moving. We aren't all scientist here so I want to explain this amazing formula in simple terms. Earlier I talked about how we knew that an atom is mainly "empty space" which is energy. We don't understand that there is so much energy locked up in the matter that surrounds us. The nucleus is of the atom is the like the sun of our solar system and it puts out radiation. It was not until Albert Einstein imagined big that all of humanity was able to understand the correlation between mass and energy. This simple algebraic formula represents the correlation of energy to matter (energy is equal to any given amount of mass).

I know many, many of us have heard this over and over and over again but have you actually sat down to think about how amazing this is? We are walking around unaware that there really is energy locked up inside of all of matter that exist. So it is known that:

* **E represents ENERGY** and energy is measured in Joules. Joules is a measurement for energy and is measured as kilograms multiplied by meters^2 per seconds^2 ($kgxm^2/s^2$). All this means is that 1 Joule of energy is equal to the force used to move an object 1 meter in the same direction as that force.

M represents MASS of the specified object. For this mathematical equation we measure the mass in Kilograms (or 1000 grams).

***C represent the SPEED OF LIGHT**. In a vacuum light has been proved to move 186,282 miles per second! So this equals 300,000,000 meters per second (for the purpose of the scientific mathematical correct measurements).

So what Einstein is expressing with his brilliant equation is that for a specific amount of mass in kilograms X the speed of light (x2) = its energy equivalence in Joules. How can you relate this to matter? Well, in one test done it has been found that one human being has the equivalence of 1.86 MILLION KILOTONS of TNT worth energy locked up inside.

All of this teachings about our vibrational frequency and our energy is not just some gibberish talk. There is scientific research that proves we are made of energy and so is everything else around us.

There are so many formulas out there in our universe. Einstein used his forever expanding imagination to figure out the theory of relativity basically explaning that everything in energy.

Here is my formula I've came up with to explain The Law of Vibration and The Law of Attraction.
$$H=ch^2$$
To see it in your hand you have to connect the head and the heart
<Insert shutterstock_573437452- image 1>
H=Hand
C=Connected
H=Head x Heart

*Basically you have to **hold it in your head, hold it in your heart** then you will **see it in your hands.***
SIMPLE ENOUGH????

What Is Stopping You
Fear?

What is it that you tell yourself? Do you tell yourself and the universe that you can't, that you don't have the money to invest, that you will fail, that the timing isn't right, that your dreams are too far out of reach and that you can't because of your family or is it that you just do not have clarity on what it is you do want? Well the universe hears all of that negative chatter in your head, what you tell yourself is what the universe will give back to you. Oh, universe says when it hears you think "I am not good enough". Then the universe says well, she or he things they are not good enough, it won't happen.

So, answer this simple question, what is stopping you? Let's say money did not exist and there were no consequences from failing, what would you be doing? Serving others? Because serving others is the one thing that human beings are able to do that will give you a reward inside!!!! Gosh this is so easy!

Say out loud: THIS IS EASY!!! Say that and believe it. Tell yourself that your dreams are worth the risk of failure but know that failure will never enter the formula for holding it in your hands.

Who Are Your Stars?
Find them and follow what they are doing.

Who has truly inspired you in life? Find them, follow them and learn how they think. Who are your pioneers? People like, Oprah Winfrey, Jim Carry, Bob Proctor, Tony Robbins, Mel Robbins, Stephen Hawking, Dr. Wayne Dyer, Eckhart Tolle, Bill Gates and I can come up with so many other names. What inspires you? Does being an inspiration inspire you? YES!!! We all should strive to be the best self we can be. BE THE BEST YOU YOU CAN BE TODAY!

Following your stars is not being paparazzi and snapping a photo of them. It's more like studying how they think. Learning from them something that you find of value to your life. It could be a simple quote or learning a new style of acting. Just do the work for free! Do not care about outcome you have in doing this study work. The more time you give to studying the more you will get back to be able to give others and that is the best compensation you can ever receive.

Shift Your Paradigm
*Significant change happens when you think
about doing something differently
Cybernetics-Subconscious*

When we start to become conscious thinkers our reality starts to look different then we start to think different. Our paradigm is our reality or how we perceive our reality to be. Paradigms come from our conscious thoughts and our subconscious thoughts. Our conscious thoughts program our subconscious thoughts. By living in the now, we become more conscious of our thoughts therefore we start to reprogram our subconscious thoughts. You see, our subconscious thoughts are kind of like the autopilot of the airplane. There is a cybernetics system in that airplane that kicks in if the plane ever veers off the path it needs to be on. That system had to be programed though by the piolet.

Tony Robbins states "If you do what you've always done, you'll get what you've always gotten." In other words explained in another way of looking at it Albert Einstein says "You can't solve a problem with the same problem that created it." When you finally start to have some understanding, your world starts to change. Some of the greatest past minds on earth have this knowledge and used it.

Our subconscious mind takes us right on the path that we have programmed it to take us every single time. We program it by thinking patters over and over that we have. For example if you have a deep subconscious thought process telling yourself you will fail at a certain class but you make a couple of good grades your subconscious kicks in, your vibration changes and you will end up failing that class because of your own autopilot subconscious mind kicking in.

If you can visualize a circle as your brain and draw a line have way horizontally across it. Write the word "conscious" on the top portion and the word "subconscious" on the lower portion on the circle. This represents your brain. Then draw a line down with a body and limbs. Make this figure look kind of like the stick man with. Thinking is the highest capability we have on this planet.

We can choose or decide what to do, this is a HUGE power that human beings hold.

The subconscious mind being like the cybernetics system it is, set on autopilot has no ability to reject thoughts and MUST accept the idea. It is our subconscious mind that cannot tell if something is real or imagined. This is studied over and over again and proven scientifically to be true. Because we can reason with situations in life, we have the ability to think. Since we are thinkers, we can control our thoughts consciously. Your conscious mind can tell your subconscious thoughts that they are CRAZY! REJECT the NEGATIVE.

Watching TV is like being hypnotized. It puts a thought right into your subconscious mind. Think about it, do it right now if someone around you is watching TV. Look at them, try getting their attention, and wave your hands in front of their face. Do they even flinch? NOPE! Not if they are deep in a movie or news report. TV puts us in a hypnotic state of mind! We go all traced out, wide eyes and not blinking. Have you ever noticed this?

Our subconscious mind is controlling our outcomes in life!!! It was programmed by someone else a long time ago, your parents or guardians. This is how you tell yourself how you see yourself, your self-image. Paradigms are formed right through your subconscious mind but now that you know this, you can shift your paradigm just by consciously becoming aware of your own thoughts. Do you want to shift your reality? Do you want to have a shift in your paradigm? Then change your thoughts!

Reprogram Your Subconscious Side

Dr. Joseph Murphy states "The subconscious mind is ruled by suggestions, it accepts all suggestions- it does not argue with you- it fulfills your wishes." Dr. Murphy studied the subconscious mind in depth, he wrote more than 30 books revolving around this understanding. He taught that we are able to heal our bodies with our minds. Not only did he teach that he also taught that we have many miracles locked inside our mind. He understood this with intense detail and wanted to spread the knowledge on this subject as one of his life purposes.

There are a few small steps in reprogramming your subconscious:

- Tell yourself positive affirmations daily
- Read, re-read and read again this book
- Use visualizations to see in your mind what you want out of life
- Meditate and Pray
- Create positive habits- yoga or staying on a routine
- Self-suggestion- start using emotions for control-feel happy
- Study this concept

How You Put Energy Out Into The Atmosphere
Positive vibrations!!!!!

You have the ability to draw energy in and also put energy out. Most of us are much unaware that we are even doing this until you become conscious of the fact that you have this ability. Somehow I understood this concept from when I was a small child. Maybe it was the fact that I was constantly told I had a tender spirit. Subconsciously, I knew that I was more than flesh. As I grew older, I had a deeper understanding of it. I learned that I was actually in control of it. I learned ways to harness my energy up so I could walk into a room and light it up. I also learned to not let those that where only seeking to feed off my energy to do so anymore- the energy vampires is what I call them. We all know some people like this, the best thing to do it just walk away from that negative mindset they are spouting out or stomp the idea they express to you right into the ground. This does not allow them to feed from your energy and effect your energy filed.

All of this may seem a bit out there for some of you to grasp, just hold on before you decide that. There has been scientific research to back my claim. We all understand that our bodies are not only flesh but are also composed of energy fields due to the "empty space" in atoms discovered. This empty space, which is most of the make up on the atom, has a massive amount of energy locked inside it. It has been studied but not fully understood that these energy particles bounce around leaping in quantum ways. What distorts or changes this energy inside our atoms? Emotions. Positive emotions like faith, hopefulness, love, passion, joy, happiness, and feeling connected. Negative emotions like rage, anger, spitefulness, envy, hopelessness and shame.

Due to our programming and DNA, some of us are termed "highly sensitive people" – which is me. From the outside senses of taste, touch, sight, smell and hearing to the inside senses of intuition, connectedness, danger, direction and so on. Some of my close friends would ask me if I was psychic at times just from being able to somehow use my range of senses to guess a birthday dead on meeting a person for the first time. It would freak the person out when I did it and my friends. Once, a guy asked me if I was a witch. NO!!!! Really? Instead, I am the woman that has to rip the tags out of her shirts, pants and underwear so they can't rub my skin a certain way. I am the girl that would not be able to handle a crowd for a long period of time, instead making my round throughout the crowd then leaving just that quick. My inner world is very complex with intense emotions. I went 5 years solid with no TV and started back doing that same thing again for the past 7 months.

Dr. Elaine Aron, a psychologist and author of *"The Highly Sensitive Person"*, studied this in detail before making her claims that this is an actual thing that some of us inherited genetically. The term "sensory processing sensitivity" is a scientific term to express being an HSP. She said "Highly sensitive people are real, we exist, and we've proven it. That alone is something to celebrate." This trait is innate. Biologist found it in over 100 species from birds, dogs, cats, horses, fruit flies and there are more. This sensitivity trait reflects a certain type of survival strategy which is being observant to conserve energy. Those of us with the trait have a different way that we are wired. I can hear the smallest of sounds across the room that nobody else pays any attention to.

Become aware that there are those of us out there being labeled as empathic or whatever you want to call it, but we all need to be aware that there is energy everywhere and we are all affected by it. We also can shift the energy of the room by putting that high intense feeling of love and positivity in our minds and bodies. It is transferable like how the scientist have proven that energy does transfer.

Here is a small scientific test you can do without anyone knowing:

- Get into a rested state with total positive feelings inside
- Self-talk – tell yourself that you will be the light in the room
- Go to a social event
- Notice that people gravitate to you- your energy is high but watch those vampires!
- Remember that you are a part of the big picture- we are one

Use The Information You Have Gathered
While you contemplate these previous ideas what questions do your thoughts offer your mind?

- Do questions arise stemming from your religious background? Who gave you that belief system? Did you decide or did someone else tell you how reality is?
- Have you questioned the authenticity of this information?
- Has the understanding of any given scientific formula in any formal educational system taught you to calculate the information in this book?
- Do you agree with the fact that you go around living day to day focused on what is right in front of you, what you can only see, taste, touch, smell or hear?
- Have you questioned yourself about how in touchy with your emotions enough to figure out how you feel right now?
- Do you feel good?
- How do you know which emotional state you are in?
- What is it that you tell yourself about yourself exactly?
- Does your mind wonder from past to the future more than being right in the moment?
- Does your paradigm tell you that we are all one?
- Are you separate from me?
- How do you serve others?
- Are you able to use visualization to imagine your desires?
- Why wait until Heaven?

- Do you think that there is a higher power source in our lives?
    - Have you started to pay attention to the way you can change the energy in the room?
- Does your vibrational alignment give you what you need?
    - Do your "Netflix" binges put unwanted ideas in your subconscious mind?
    - Will we eventually crack the code in knowing the TRUE understanding of E=mc^2
- How many things do you believe that are not true?

Abracadabra! But it's Not Magic!

"As Above, So Below"- The Magician- Hermetic Concept (you will learn in part 3)
"These higher faculties we've got are like magic" Bob Proctor
Abracadabra by itself means "What you say becomes" or "I will create as I speak"

Our words create reality. Do you say you are depressed? Do you tell yourself you are depressed? How can you when you have your own will? Do you want to feel depressed? What negative thoughts do you keep spinning in your mind? When you say you are depressed then you are depressed. I a person in unable to see their future, unable to imagine and visualize, you think your life is never going to change. Holding on to the past causes us to get depressed. Because we have to tendency to identify through our past experiences we tend to define ourselves by our past achievements and our past hurt and our past whatever. The truth is this moment now is the only thing that really exist. Quit being emotionally involved with your past situations. By you telling yourself anything, you create it for yourself. Understand this, have faith. Do not choose fear over faith.

Focusing on sickness only amplifies the sickness. Instead while your body is undergoing some type of illness focus on everything around you that you are grateful for. Start appreciating the parts of your body that you appreciate. Appreciate your eyes for seeing, your skin for protecting your body and start appreciating the parts of you that you consider to have wellbeing.

Instead of being a sick being you will become a being that is in wellbeing. Do this repetitively, and over time watch how your body will heal itself.

Do you say to yourself that things cannot be done? Then that is what you will get. Do you say to yourself that it can be done? Then that is what you will get. Do you curse your future? Or Do you bless your future? This word "abracadabra" is used by magicians but the word is much older and basically means when you say something then you will get it.

Wellbeing, Human Being, Just Being
Does the body have more value than the mind?

Since as far back as you can remember do you recall getting a cut and asking for a Band-Aid? Do you recall learning that brushing your teeth twice a day is necessary to prevent decay? But...what did you learn about maintaining your psychological health? Think far back to childhood, do you agree that our bodies are valued more than our mental state of being? What do you teach your children about emotional hygiene? What about mental decay? Do you teach your children how to cope with failure, loneliness or rejection? These mental injuries can also get worse with no care. Why is it that our physical health is so much more important than our mental health?

How about doing the work to understand how to take care of your mental health to create balance in for your overall wellbeing. First of all knowing that you are never alone is the most important thing to understand. You are not set apart from me and I am not set apart from you. We are both in this world together and not separate from one another really. In fact, my thoughts are effecting yours at this very moment.

Learning how to be in the moment is being. Just being is an important aspect to being a human being and in being we have a state of wellbeing. What is just being? Being in the moment, putting that cell phone down and laying in the grass with your children is being. Being is noticing the birds singing outside your window when your eyes first open in the morning. Being is being appreciative for what you do have. Being is being conscious of your own thoughts. Are you a human being that is just being or do you have some sort of suffering going on? Are you hanging on to the past? Are you having restlessness about the future? Depression is not being able to let go and anxiety is about being worried about your future. The past and the present.

In the state of wellbeing, this is when you are in your limitless state. Our limitless state of wellbeing is being present right now. Being well takes doing the work to bridge the gap between your body and your mind. Wellbeing is a human being just being. Why are you called a human being?

<u>Depression Comes From Not Understanding</u>

How do you view yourself? What is your self-image? Do you understand that your own self-image is linked to being in a depressed state? Do you know that if you are having negative thoughts about yourself then you slip into a depression? Our self-image we hold in our minds eye about ourselves is shaped by many different past expirees we had. Rather the past experiences be good, like a degree, or bad, like being taken advantage of. As we are holding on to the past to gain a sense of identity keeps your mind in that same sense of being. You hold that same vibration, like handcuffs on your wrist everywhere you go.

The degree, the positive accomplishments only do the same thing to your identity. You relate to your past to identify yourself and hold a self-image for yourself. In doing that we also form the habit of not letting do all the bad that happened in our past as well. We decide we are our past instead of deciding we are our future or we are the moment.

It's so true once you gain a simple understanding that your self-talk, self-image comes from your past. So here is the paradigm shift that needs to take place in your life: know that the moment is ONLY who you are now but the future is WHERE you will be going. Hold yourself in alignment with that and that is when your world will being to take a turn. It is so simple but so many do not understand this concept because we a programmed to think

51

that our past shapes who we are and that who we are is who we will ever be.

Depression only is comes from what it is that you tell yourself. Do you like yourself?

Get in front of the mirror and repeat to yourself that you like yourself. Do this every single day. Sound silly, right? I can tell you I do this and I am not ashamed of it because it makes me feel good. Find something to appreciate about yourself. Write it down on a piece of paper and stick it beside your mirror in the bathroom. Focus on healing your mental state. Know like you know like you know that your future will change! Expect it! You will start to be positive more naturally and drawing more interesting people into your life. Everything starts with yourself. Work on this and create a new belief system for yourself which in turn you change your subconscious mind autopilot choices.

If you are telling yourself that you are not able to do this, then that is what you will get. If you tell yourself that you can do this, then that is what you will get. Understand????YES! Say you do.

Anxiety is Suppression
Women are affected by anxiety on a ratio of 2:1 verses men
OUR INSULA

The Insula is an amazing part of the brain. This lightly understood area in the brain has some major effects on our bodies. This region of our brains is there area that our emotions flow from. Emotions like empathy, inspiration, love, hate, joy, in rage, fear, faith, guilt, disgust, pride, humiliation, connectedness or atonement. It is why we have an emotional response to a song, a song that may bring you back to a certain time in your life. It also reads body states like hunger and craving and it is what makes you reach for that snack at midnight. Let that sink in for a minute. Think about it, our emotions come from a tiny area in the brain? What do our emotions do? They actually have power over all of your actions. Have you ever smelled a sent that gave you the same emotions as what you were doing when you first smelt it?

When this area was studied on this area in our brains staid lit up when scanned for longer periods of time with women. Where as in men, when this area lit up when felling an emotion it did light up but didn't stay lit like how women's brain did. The men were able to go on and focus on who to solve the problem. So women may feel empathy for others more than men do, men seem to have a better ability to compartmentalize things (which means that they are not able to just move on the next thing without solving the issue first). In the insula women are able to relate for a longer period of time to a certain situation than men but they are able to push issues aside without solving the problem. I thought this was very interesting. This may be why women are feeling more anxious than men. But maybe we all have an aspect as a feminine and masculine inside of us? Basically the study done shows that women have more anxiety because they suppress issues more so than men do.

<u>Disease Turns into Decay</u>

Since fear is the main root to anxiety. Fear puts our bodies in a unstable vibration. When our body is in an unstable vibration we only get back more of that vibration just by the universe law. So many people run out and get prescribed PROZAC to decrease their depression and anxiety. When really what they should be doing is practicing to learn how to be more conscious of their own thoughts knowing you can tell yourself anything. How do you get rid of fear? Face it, just that simple.

Make a decision that you can eliminate fear right out of your life. Fear is only an emotional state steaming from doubt and worry. Face your fear and fear will leave you. You can control your attitude, your thoughts, your feelings and your actions. Just make a conscious decision to refuse to have fear rule your life anymore.

When our bodies are held in the frequency of fear, it calls that same emotional vibration that comes back to us. The universe says what you tell it to allow. When your body is in a state of dis-ease then your body will manifest a disease. Now, this depends on what you would consider disease. When we are in a states of

53

wellbeing that is when the universe says back to us we are being well. If you are holding yourself in alignment with fear, then let it go and walk into an unknown zone in life and know that the universe will only allow you to fly. You have to just have faith. In other words you have to trust that things are always working out for you.

Go From Understanding To Being Emotional About it- Faith

Since our emotions control our actions, begin to already feel some emotions linked to your desires in life. If it is a relationship you want then start to live like you already have that relationship instead of being in a vibrational state of resistance about it. When you want something too much your body will put a vibration of resistance out. You have to want it, know it is coming and then let it go- just know like you know that it will come back to you.

For an example when a Hawk teaches it's young to fly the mother will fly to another tree and sit there and call for her young. She will call and call and call for the baby bird to fly there unitl the baby bird actually does. She has faith that the baby bird will fly to her instinctively. This is how we should treat everything in our life.

Today while I was on a beach walk with my puppy I practiced this. I let her off her leash, and let her just run. I let her explore far away from me and held a thought strong and started to believe she would come back no matter what. It's like I held her on a vibrational leash. She'd disappear for a few minutes and then she'd come right back to me. Play with this today with anything you feel resistance to.

Have you ever been on a new car lot and the sales person pushes a little too hard? What did that make you do? You didn't want that car did you? This same thing happens in almost every situation in life. You meet resistance. When you do meet resistance in life what do you do about it? Do you persist? Or do you back away and turn around going in that same direction you have gone before? When you want to reach a goal in life and you have a bump in the road do you just give up or do you have faith that it will work out?

James Allen has a famous quote that reads "Mind is master power that molds and makes, and we are mind, and evermore we take the tool of thought, and shaping what we will, bringing forth a thousand joys, a thousand ills. We think in secret, and it comes to pass- Our world is but our looking glass." Pretty genius how this was stated.

Chose Fear Over Faith?

"When I die, when my coffin is being taken out
You must never think I am missing this world. Don't
shed any tears, don't lament or fell sorry
I'm not falling into a monster's abyss. When
you see my course is being carried
Don't cry for my leaving, I am not leaving
I'm arriving at eternal love "–
Rumi

That poem from Rumi is so full of insight. In this full poem he also states "when you leave me in the grave, don't say goodbye, remember a grave is only a curtain for the paradise behind." In this poem he has many lessons that most of us need to understand. Why fear anything when our universe will not let you fall unless you believe it will. When we die we do not die, our spirit lives on for all of eternity. Your life is full of judgement you place on yourself and identify with. Our goal is to have you understand that all you have to do it let those negative self judgements go and have faith instead of fear in life.

Rumi also compares sunset and dawn to their being an end and beginning to things. He says "you'll only see me descending into a grave, now watch me rise, how can there been an end when the sun sets or the moon goes down?" And then he goes on saying "It looks like the end, it seems like a sunset but in reality it is a dawn, when the grave locks you up that is when your soul is free'd."

There is more to our life than just the physical. What we see, taste, smell, touch and hear are only just a part of what reality is. Use your emotions to get the results you want from anything in life.

If its weight loss, hold in your mind the vision of what you will look like, have faith in that vision. Also instead having the emotional reaction of fear when you've failed at something terribly, just trust that the universe is showing you which direction you should go in and trust that it is the better path for you.

The poem that Rumi wrote goes on and states "Have you ever seen a seed fallen to the earth not rise with a new life, why should you doubt the rise of a seed named human." Which that is a powerful line but then he says "Have you ever seen a bucket lowered into a well coming back empty, why lament for a soul when it can come back like Joseph from the well." Joseph from the well is from Genesis 37- you must read that.

The last verse in the poem says "when for the last time you close your mouth your words and soul will belong to the world of no place no time." You soul ends up in a place of an abundant source of love, which God is love. Face your fears and choose faith over fear. Know you will fly!

Creation Over Disintegration
When you are creating, you are rejuvenating your soul

So, one of our main ways to live in a state of mental health is having some sort of creative outlet in life. I've heard it through out my years people say "you're so creative" and "I am not creative" or "I don't have any artistic abilities" and on and on. It goes back to self-talk. What do you tell yourself? We are creations from a higher being that moves in us, through us, is us and is outside of us. We have a source of creative energy that surrounds us daily. The problem is, is that some people are not tapped into how amazing it feels to create something and practice doing it over and over. It does not matter if you are not good at it! It does not matter if you will practice and still not be good at it. If you enjoy doing it, do it and create anything.

Creating a scientific formula is not a form of art but it is still creating. Not everything that is a type of creation is art. Think about it. Do you like to bake? Do you like to braid hair? Do you like to fix old machines? Do you like to do surgery? Do you like to sing in your car? ANYTHING you do and think is a creation.

It is once we stop creating that our bodies start to wilt like a flower that has no water. Our thoughts and emotions drive our actions. Doing what makes you feel good will always bring you to a state of mental health. Even when you are 107 years old, learn something new so that your brain never stops creating or so that you never stop feeling love from creation of some sort.

If you are just being, getting still and really being conscious of your thoughts, this is when our highest sense of creation comes. It's a energy that pulses through you, it's when that painting that you painted did not come from you. It came from a source outside of you that you aligned with to receive and allowed to flow through you.

"Your life is your art. What are you creating today?" The Universe

Will You Overcome Depression?
You were born to direct your thoughts by paying attention to the way you are feeling.

If you are aware that you are having an emotionally bad period of time, what you are saying to the universe, without even knowing it, is I've been so focused on the PROBLEM that I am out of reach from the SOLUTION. You cannot find a solution when you are waste deep in the problem. We cannot fix the problem with the same thought process that got us to that problem. You have got to find some way of putting some distance between you and the problem. I am talking about finding a different vibrational frequency. This means, walk away, change the channel, go get a pedicure, hang around different friends, make list of positive aspects, make a list of affirmations, sleep more, exercise more, say to yourself you only have 5 seconds to make a choice, meditate every day, take a long bubble bath, play the guitar- you get my point. Instead of dragging your head around laying in the bed all day focused on the depression, re-direct your focus! Get focused on what will put you in the feeling of love, abundance, joy, peace, motivation, excitement, thankfulness and all of those good feeling emotions that we experience in life.

If you are aware that you have been FEELING more depressed that you are FEELING happy or more overwhelmed that enthusiastic or more in rage than more balanced what this means is YOU HAVE BEEN LETTING the environment around you train you into an alignment that is NOT NATURAL to you. Yes, you have been allowing this to happen by not paying attention and CARING about the way you feel. You see, all it takes is saying to yourself on a conscious level that you deserve to feel good. ALLOW yourself to just feel good and be happy, just be happy, just be. When you allow this natural alignment of pure love and happiness flow to you, in you and through you is when your life starts to take some simple but amazing twist and turns. You have allowed yourself to receive all the abundance that is in this world flow to you. It is good for you to FEEL GOOD.

Do you understand that you are not only flesh and blood? Do you understand that there is more to your atoms that make up the matter we call flesh? Do you understand that there is energy flowing to you, in you, through you EVERY SINGLE DAY? Do you receive this message with gratitude? Do you know that you have a spirit? Do you understand that you hold a vibrational frequency that attracts to you that same frequency everywhere you go? Do connect with your emotions? Do you connect with your spiritual self? DO you understand that you are more than what you can see, taste, touch, feel and hear? Do you know that when your life gets better and better that it is ALWAYS because you are forward looking?

By forward looking you are not looking back to the past and holding on to that which was instead of holding on the idea of that which will be!!! It is just so simple and we ALL know this instinctively but somewhere in our programming we were taught to not see it this way. In fact we were not taught this at all. We were not taught to even take a glimpse of this in our educational systems. Are you hung up on your reality that exist? Well in doing so, you ignore the vibrational alignment that parallel with that vibration you are in. Yes, it is right there beside you at all times you just have to become aware that it is there. Get hung up on what will be and are as human beings.

Do not say that the money you have in your bank account
is what is, say to yourself that money is what was! This is so
true! The money that you see in your bank account is there only
because of what you did to put it there. It is not what is now! It
is what was! Do you get it? What is – is this spiritual vibration
of who you are right now- do not hang around in who you were.
Move forward, more forward, more forward and CASH in your
vibrational alignment of what is and what will be. Want to find a
NEW addiction? FIND the addiction of feeling good. It is amazing.
You will amaze yourself with the things that will start to flow in your
life so fast. Now, some of these things will come fast to you and
others not so fast but do not ever hang around in who you were.
Reach out, reach forward, hold that vision in your mind and feel it
in your heart then you will see it in your hands.

Problems Are Opportunities
"And not only so, but we glory in tribulations also:
Knowing that tribulation worketh patience;
And patience, experience: and experience, hope:"
Romans 5:3-5 (KJV)

My son is now 11 years old and lives with his dad full time by
his choice. The way child custody is regulated in our society is
inhumane in my opinion. We take our grief and bad decisions out
on our children forcing them to stay with one parent or the other
by a judge of the court. Now given I know that every situation
in different. If a child is unsafe with the other parent is one thing
but if the child is taken away from a perfectly sane mother and
the father is given full custody is torture on many levels for that
woman. Women are not the only ones having to face this problem.
Many men lose full custody and their children are meant to stay
with mom and go with dad only every other weekend. The children
develop relationships with friends and other family members in
their life that they are attached to and forced by the other parent
to go to the others house even if they are laying on the floor crying
wanting to stay with mom or dad.

I dealt with this in the best loving way I knew how to because it hurt my heart knowing he was not enjoying his time with me anymore and that he'd rather be in the comfort of a consistent routine. I would never force my son to come with me if he didn't want to. I would never impose disrespect to his life in that way, my decisions are not his problem. Once my son started to get older, he didn't need me so much anymore, he wanted his father more and I understood. He has a whole life that I am not a part of away from my life. Although this is the best for my son's life at first when he started to not want to come with me so much, it caused a HUGE problem for me personally in my heart.

There were many tugs of war that went on. Tugs of war emotionally and I felt empty inside. I relate it to having "empty nest" syndrome prematurely, way prematurely. This wasn't supposed to happen until he was a college age student. My heart was breaking inside for him. When he started to pull back from me he was around the age of 7 years old. He had his bedroom all set up as if he lived with me full time, I'd walk by it and it would be empty. No children energy in my home anymore but somehow instinctively I knew this was the best thing for him. He is happy. He is in a special program for children that achieve high scores academically and is one of the most tender and polite child that I know. He always will be my son and nobody will ever take that away from me.

During the first years that he was pulling away from me was so hard. Then, about two years ago, I started to see it in a different light. I started to just let go of what happened in the past and trusted in motherly instincts for my situation. I saw it as an opportunity to go back to school! I had more alone time and time outside of work to focus on working towards some personal goals. Yes, at 36 years old, I went back to college to get that degree I never got. I looked at my problem in a different way. Instead of focusing so much on the problem, my child custody situation, I just let it go, knew where I stood with myself, love, my son and with the higher powers of this universe. I knew what my intentions were and so a rocket of desire shot off. That desire is still going and will never ever ever leave my life.

I've always said every situation happens for a reason. Problems happen to us so that you live can through them to be able to help others in their way in life with similar problems. It is to serve the greater energy source of this universe. It is to serve others.

Some problems are not easy to talk about, there are stereotypes attached to mothers that do not have their children. I am here to tell you know that a stereotype is all that it is. Every situation is different, every problem is different, and every outcome is different. What will stay the same is the fact that when you look at your problem as an opportunity, you will achieve great things.

Repetition Creates Your Paradigm

When you focus on an idea with great passion you start to realize in that focusing you feel good. When you feel good you want more of what is making you feel good. Positive thinking is something that you have to reprogram your mind to start to do. It takes practice and it takes studying how to be a positive thinker. Most of us are on a true automatic thinking mode, we let negative ideas enter our subconscious not even paying attention that you are doing so. It you tell yourself something over and over and over again then you will shape that for your life it doesn't matter if it's good or bad. THIS IS SO IMPORTANT TO UNDERSTAND.

Telling yourself that you have no way of getting that house you desire only will get that for you. If you tell yourself that there is nothing else more for your life over and over and over again then you will not have anything more for your life. If you tell yourself that you will be a millionaire in the next 5 years over and over and over again then you will be a millionaire in the next 5 years. It is such a simple concept.

Which one do you want? Do you want to be stuck in the same repetitive thinking and doing that you have now? Does that make you feel good? OR Do you want to have a desire and tell yourself you will have that desire over and over again to see it in your hands in the future? Do you want to change your repetitive thinking patters?

61

One thing that I have done and many other people that have shifted there paradigm is find a mentor that teaches you this concept and listen to them every day, read their book every day. Doing this helps you to form new ideas and concepts in your mind. Another thing to do that I have done is to make a sign that has the words "I am _____" on it and hang it by your bathroom mirror. Now, some people may think you've gone crazy but that is OK. You know you haven't. You will start to see your mind shift into a positive mindset and your world change quickly when you start to practice this. When you say to yourself "I am a future millionaire" and you look in the mirror, you create emotion inside. Listen to your hearts intentions. Look into your own brown, blue or green eyes and say, "I am a leader" or "I am valuable" or "I create contrast". Do that daily, multiple times a day when you go in the bathroom, when you brush your teeth, when you take a shower, when you are putting your makeup on.

There is one more important thing that have proven results in changing your reality is writing your goals down and looking at them several times a day. Doing this repetitive action of looking at your goals over and over creates an emotional response in your heart. You think about getting there and it makes you tingle all over. Hold that vibration there….hold it there and you will achieve your dreams.

Anybody Could Have Anything They Want
Thoughts create things

Tony Robbins, a well-respected motivational speaker said "Whatever you hold in your mind on a consistent basis is exactly what you will experience in your life." This holds much truth to it. Tony Robbins is not the only one that knows this truth. So many before him knew this, but its not having the knowledge behind it that creates understanding. It is having the imagination to match the facts. We all know what the great Albert Einstein said about imagination being the key component to any future manifestations. We must practice this understanding every single day of our lives to reach the highest potential of who you are.

We've all heard the quote "Do not die with the music still inside." This gives perspective to the understanding that anyone can have anything they desire out of life. We are born to have abundance in our life. What do you accept for the truth for yourself? Do you accept that what you are creating in your life is you? If you are not growing money from the seeds you've planted then you are creating a more prosperous you. There are no limits to the ways that you can create, nothing is ever truly completed, all things can be changed. You can have it all, you can have anything you desire.

Your Three Wishes

We've all heard the story about the genie in the bottle and the tree wishes you can have from rubbing on that genie lamp. Do you know the origins of this story? The story goes back to years and years ago. The word Genie comes from the word Jinn. Jinn are basically spirits and this story evolved to genie due to it being the related to the genius. This word is very very very old and predates to before when people were practicing Islam. People believed spirits were attached to buildings. These spirits, jinn's- genies, were said to be genius because of their powers they hold. As you can imagine since the stories are so old, they have morphed into a jinn being a genie like seen in Aladdin. When you research the story it says nothing about having only three wishes. The wishes are actually endless.

Actually the belief in Jinn still exist. The concept that Jinn are spirits that were created before man kind and they are only spiritual energy. There are said to be good and bad Jinn. The fact is that we all know that we are spiritual beings and that something outside of us is greater than us. As in with all religions and belief systems, they all tie together in one way or another. Jinns are like angles and demons. Stories get twisted over time but mainly know there is a source outside of us, there is a God, and there is a higher power that is unseen.

Abraham Lincoln said "To believe in the things you can see and touch is no belief at all but to believe in the unseen is a triumph and a blessing." One of America's great leaders understood this simple truth. There is more to life than the physical.

Draw Closer To What You Want By Your Thoughts
"Rule your mind or it will rule you." Buddha

Buddha held great insight into knowing that our brains have a subconscious and a conscious mind. As one of our world's great leaders he taught so many aspects of this when he spoke. He also said "No one saves us but ourselves. No one can and no one may. We ourselves must walk the path." Buddha talked about peace coming from within and taught to not seek peace from the outside senses. "The mind is everything. "What you think, you become" is another valuable quote of his and really they are endless. He was the motivational speaker of his day. We all need to learn to think like Buddha.

We must apply the knowledge passed down to us to our lives. In learning that we are in control of how we direct our thoughts we can do anything. Drawing closer to the goals you've created for yourself feels so good and why not feel good? "There is no path to happiness, happiness is the path."- Buddha.

Part 2
Operating Being Conscious: Are you on automatic thinking mode?

Change Your Life By Waking Up An Hour Early
Reprogramming your mind

Not a morning person? Try to push yourself to be. Is this is not in your comfort zone? You'd rather sleep in to 9am? 10am? 12am? and stay up late? Do you have to be at work by 9am? Get up at 7am? Try to wake up at 6am instead. You give yourself an extra hour to accomplish goals! Having that extra hour gives you time to be more productive! I never have a full basket of laundry since I have been doing this. Some people want to use this extra hour for a morning time work out. For me, I wanted the extra hour to focus on reaching my goals I have set for myself like writing this book. So, this is a simple solution to having not being able to give myself the excuse that I did not have enough time.

At first, it is not so easy but then it gets so easy that you will even want to wake up early on the weekends. Your natural circadian rhythm starts to kick in and you will just be a natural early riser. When we have a balanced circadian rhythm our brains are balanced. The chemicals in our brain are more regulated when we have a normal bed time routine and morning routine. These facts have been scientifically proved. Like with any lifestyle change you can give yourself break days if you need to like staying up late for a special occasion or sleeping in on the weekends. I would suggest to not sleep in too late on the weekends though because our bodies do get out of rhythm easy and it really does affect our body.

I used **Mel Robbins** 5 second rule and it REALLY does work! If you have not heard of this rule it is a simple rule to grab concept of. She says to stop hitting the snooze button and instead when your alarm goes off count to 5 and just get up. She teaches us how nobody ever feels like it and you may never feel like it but we have a choice and control of our bodies with our minds. Mel says "Count 5, 4, 3, 2, 1 then shoot up like a rocket!" Let your rockets of desire sore when you use her 5 second rule. She also says "The moment you have an instinct to act on a goal, you must physically move within 5 seconds or your brain will stop you. 5, 4, 3, 2, 1 GO!" This worked for me because I needed to hear that nobody really feels like it. Now I understand how great getting up an hour early each day can be for production and achieving your personal goals.

Use the 5 Second Rule

This "5 second rule" Mel Robbins uses really does set the stage for so many more things to take shape for your future. Not only does it help your mind take shape but it helps your body take shape. You will feel like you are making progress. When you start to feel like you are making progress then you start to feel good and then there that is! Like a rocket of desire, your vibration becomes higher, more positive and you will do get things.

The old you lives in the autopilot lifestyle. When you start to apply the lessons taught in this book your brain will not be on autopilot anymore. You will have complete control on how you train yourself to work towards some amazing things in your life. The new you then becomes more confident and courageous. As you apply the 5 second rule to anything in your life, not just waking up early then you won't allow fear to stop you from getting that new job position that you've always wanted.

When you train your subconscious mind to think in terms of knowing that we live in a fast pace universe then you will not let that idea slip through your fingers and watch someone make it happen instead. You will be the one to make it happen. It does taking stepping out of your comfort zone though. You will not feel like doing it, push yourself and know it will be worth it in the end. Give yourself a 21 challenge to use this thought process in your everyday life instead of just letting your subconscious thoughts take control of your actions.

Trust The Process
Trust the process, your life won't change in day, practice patience, it takes time.

If you held a key ring in your pocket with a few main keys for success, patience would be on one of those keys. Persistence would be on another one of those magical keys. "Practice patience: it is the essence of praise. Have patience, for that is true worship. No other worship is worth as much. Have patience; patience is the key to all relief" said the wise Rumi. It is well known that having the patience to allow a new way of doing something become habit is not the most comfortable thing but it is vital in transformation.

Carl Jung states "Until you make the unconscious conscious, it will direct your life and you will call it fate." He is basically saying if you let your mind take you where it will, you will say you had no control over any given situation or outcome. Once you gain awareness and wake up to the fact that you are directing your mind and your mind directs your actions then you will make these changes needed for the most abundance lifestyle you can imagine up. Have faith that you're going to be led by a serious of unknown circumstances to get from where you are now to where you will be. You must not give up half way in the process.

Have you ever been lost looking for a place you needed to be? Well, did you just give up and go back home? Did you just say, I can't find it and do a U turn in the road to go back home? NO!! You wouldn't quit looking until you found it. You may have stopped to ask someone for directions or trusted your GPS to take your there instead. The point is when you choose to go somewhere and if you have not made it there yet due to a detour then do not give up.

You must trust that there will be tiny little events that will tie in your goal to become into reality.

"Have patience. Wait until the mud settles and the water is clear. Remain unmoving until right action arises by itself" Lao Tzu-Tao Teh Ching. This concept of trusting the process is not anything new and has been taught in various ways throughout history. Patience must be practiced and it arises from our emotions. Our emotions are tied into how we can become a patient person that trust the process. "Be completely humble and gentle, be patient, bearing with one another in love" Ephesians 4:2. Clarity in holding that vision close to your heart and faith in knowing that things will fall into place exactly how you want them to be are the outcome of you trusting the process.

Trust It
"The Law of Obedience"

You are the master of your faith. As you gain knowledge you have a choice on what to do with this knowledge. The facts have no meaning to your life unless you are able to hold faith close to your heart. Being obedient to faith will open a door of wisdom instead of ignorance for the rest of your life. Success or failure is chosen depending on how strong your faith is. What do you believe? What have you been studying? What have you been believing? Have you been obedient to the divine Law of Obedience?

"Obey my voice, and I will be your God, and ye shall be my people" **Jer. 7:23**. Every person that obeys the divine Laws of the universe is truly a servant of God and a servant to others by doing so. By doing so you will gain a greater purpose for your life and reap power to direct every condition and allow blessings galore!!!! AMEN TO THAT! This is the truth. As you read further along The Law of Obedience will begin to really make sense for its lesson for the world outside of you but more so for the world inside of you.

As we look to nature for the answers, something outside ourselves, we can begin to understand this truth inside our souls. In part one of this book I discussed how we can plant seeds of ideas and water them by our thoughts. Well, in nature when you plant a seed you also have to be obedient to the laws of nature. Mother Nature has no problems without offering the solution. Mother Nature has no burdens that she cannot carry. Why we ask? There is a law of harmony and order and she must be obedient to it because there is no other way. If a little young baby seed happens to sprout in the winter time, Mother Nature will kill it with the freeze. This unruly sprout has not obeyed Mother Nature. A seed cannot sprout during a winter freeze. Yet, in her all mighty grace that same blanket of ice that killed off the sprout serves as a blanket of warmth for the soil and seedlings underneath it obeying the law. If a person decides to grow a garden they must obey with nature's law. When the law is obeyed then there is a garden that has flourished with wondrous fruits. So take this law of the earth and apply it to the laws of the universe, the universe you have inside of you.

Mistakes are made often when we put the laws of nature at the top instead of the laws of the spirit first. Peter and the apostils taught that "We must obey God rather than man." Which means we must obey our spiritual guides before we obey the ways of men. We must give in and become a servant to the unseen rather than the seen. Instead of worshiping what you can hear, see, smell, taste, touch we must worship what your soul senses inside, what you feel, and the higher power all around us.

Think about materialistic things you gain on this earth as being loaned to you instead. We do not own anything really. God loans them to us. All that you are loaned to you is according to your understanding of the law he serves. We are all born naked and we all die in that same nakedness. All of the earthy materialistic things are stripped away from you, even this worldly burdens you carry. What burdens are you carrying? Look at them close and find out what you understand about this law of obedience.

Do your burdens come from an idea of some type of possession you have in life? Do you have children that you carry a burden for? Well even our children are not ours. Every child was born into this world a spiritual being and we leave this earth the same. We are not owned by our father or mother but we were given to them for this earth but not to have. They do not take us when they pass on to a spirit without their body nor, do they take anything else with them. We do not really own our children just the same. They have an earthy father and mother to teach them the correct laws of life so they can fulfill their earthy duties but they also have a heavenly father and mother just the same. Does this make sense to you?

My father, Irvin Rozier, a great man in so many ways said he knew this all along while raising us with no mother in the house hold. He said he trusted that God would lead our ways in life, he really trusted that completely. He said he knew he didn't own us, we weren't his to have but only came to him as gifts and lessons in life. He talked about his prayers for us in the past and even now as we are all grown. He is obedient to God and as a great gardener/ farmer can grow amazing crops just by following the law of nature. As we obey the law, trust that is the truth, we do not obey fear any longer. We begin to trust it, trust the law, trust that the higher power on this planet moves to us, in us and through us.

Giving V/S Receiving
*"We make a living by what we get. But we make
a life by what we give."- Winston Churchill*

Everything is constantly on the move in our universe. This motion is a cause from the result of our consciousness that results in the expression of diversity in our universe. Currency means to run or flow, it is a symbol of constant flow or exchange. Currency is also our word for money. If your intention is to hoard your money, you will stop the flow of money coming into your life. Welcome to the Law of Giving and Receiving.

Keep the flow of ideas circulating in the world. Every relationship is a flow of give and take. If you are giving then something will always come back to you. If you just live your life in a giving mode, your life will always be richer. It may not be in the form that you gave it but it will always come back to you in some way. Pay attention to the words you give out, the ideas you put out. So many of us are really good at the giving part but during the receiving in we are not so good at it and we won't allow it at times. We have been taught along the way that it's better to give than to receive. It actually works both ways, balance is needed in all things to have ....well... balance.

To be opened to receiving you have to be sincere and opened. You also have to be able to appreciate and be grateful for what has been given to you. Understand that whatever is given to you is not something you have earned but rather it is something that has been freely given to you by the universe. If you do a job for someone and they insist on paying you, if you resist it then you are actually making an imbalanced situation happen. You have disrupted the flow of circulating energy. Just allow yourself to receive whatever it is.

Before you clock in for your shift for the day, tell the universe thank you for this day and offer a loving energy from your heart sincerely. Make this a habit on a daily basis giving thanks for the opportunity that has been given to you. Learn to silently bless those around you with love in life. I've put into practice this giving by bringing donuts to the office on Friday mornings or when my gut tells me to. It's a small act that cost around $7.00 and makes the last day of the week that much easier to get through. It does not have to be with anything materialistic, you can just offer positive thoughts in your surroundings. Watch what happens when you start to practice this.

Today, try start the circulation of joy with your thoughts. Be open to receiving gifts from others rather it be in the form of something that is materialistic, money, a prayer or a compliment. Make it a point to keep the wealth circulating in your life by giving and receiving our lives most precious gifts. The gifts of caring, accepting, appreciation and love are some great gifts to give and receive. Each time you find yourself in a conversation silently wish them peach, joy and happiness in their lives.

Most of my patient's will never know that when this nurse is wrapping their wound that I am also silently saying a prayer for their healing while my hands are touching their wound. I have always done this through my years of being a nurse. I have not told anyone that I do this though because it is a personal silent give I choose to give without any acknowledgment for knowing at the same time that there is a law here and it is the law of giving and receiving.

<u>Guide Your Thoughts</u>
*Romans 12:2 "Do not conform to the pattern
of this world, but be transformed
By the renewing of your mind"*

When you look in the mirror you will see a body, a molecular stricter made of matter. You cannot see your spiritual being, that of which what life arises from. If you want to change the results in your life, you have to begin to tap into that which is inside us, our minds. We have a conscious and subconscious mind. The subconscious mind has no ability to reject anything we tell it. It's a massive part of why we do the things we do. Our bodies are only that vessel that our minds use to create action, it's the instrument of our minds. When you see a body moving in a certain direction, what you are really seeing is the expression of what is going on in the mind.

Knowing our minds have this subconscious that will never reject and only accept we have to understand the impact that it has on our overall wellbeing of life. Our bodies are in vibration according to the thoughts we are having. Maybe you've never known this or understand this reading this now. Look at your hand, yes its solid but what else? It's a mass of atoms that have created molecules that have an enormous high speed vibration. This is absolutely not science fiction. Not only that did you know you have the ability to alter the vibration that your body is in? The vibration that your body is in right now is expressed in how you are feeling. If you ask someone right now how they feel and they say they don't feel well, you can know that they have been in a vibration that is expressed from negative thinking. If you ask another person how they feel and they say they feel great then you should understand that they are only expressing the vibration that comes from positive thinking.

We control our feeling by the images we hold in our consciousness and hand over to our subconsciousness. Try doing this, see yourself very wealthy. See in your mind that you are driving your dream car, dressed in the best of clothing, living in a fine house by the water, socializing with classy people and you are able to take the best of vacations. You visualize an amazing life for yourself. Your subconscious mind cannot tell reality from fiction. Do this on a regular bases and see what manifest in your world. Let those visualizations sink into your subconscious mind by feeling the emotions attached to how those outer world things make you feel. It is the images that you impress on your subconscious mind that controls the vibration you are in right now!

Hold the image in your mind and hold it in your heart then you will see it in your hands! This works every time without any glitches. Our subconscious mind is powerful! And WE have control over it! Direct your thoughts by seeing your life the way you would see your life if you could have anything you'd ever want in this world. We all have different desires, what is yours?

Instead of Digging Down, Rise Up
Lift people up to their potential and higher self
"Love is the great miracle cure. Loving ourselves works
MIRACLES in our lives." Louise Hay

God or Source, ultimate love energy, or whatever you refer to the higher power in life only allows to see the positive aspects of one another in each other. Whenever our thoughts are tuned in, tapped in, turned on to this ultimate love energy, this source energy, God, the higher power in our life it is then we are in alignment with who we really are. The truth is that when you are able to find harmony and balance between you and you then you will have any other harmony that is possible. So, if you allow this state of harmony between you and you it is possible to find alignment with others even when there is an argument that occurs. It is now, at this time when we find that perfect expansion and connected to God. When we reach for that which is outside of ourselves to feel better it is then that we are not being aligned with this ultimate love source.

When we lean into food for pleasure, alcohol for escape, drugs for depression treatment, acceptance by others for confirmation or love from another for the love we need we will never learn how to be tuned in, tapped in and turned on to that source which flows freely to us, in us and through us. The feeling of love and joy comes from thoughts we are able to consciously be aware of and create in our conscious state of thinking. It is then that the emotions flow to us through the thoughts that we are allowing ourselves to imagine.

Unconditional love means holding love in your being no matter what condition takes place. While you are loving others regardless of their past or their present you are allowing yourself to uplift their inner self. In the meantime, you've risen above any condition in order to send those loving thoughts and gifts out into the universe. Every single time you do that, you help others line up with their true self. This may be hard to do when you are so conditioned to categorize everything in your reality. By categorizing people we but distance between the main premise that we all are one in this universe. Not understanding this truth will only create distance between you and yourself as the reflective vibration you receive back. Get over beating up on yourself then you are able to get over beating up on others.

What Is a Pain Body?

Accumulation of old emotional pain that either you had
In your past or that generations before you had
that you carry in your energy field.

Pain can be an addiction for some of us and for others that do not have the addiction to the pain body still will feed it regularly without even realizing what we are doing. We create drama for ourselves so that we can feel that pain again. Some people have a larger pain body than others and others have a smaller pain body. This pain body is linked to our own past painful memories, past down generations of family pains and it can be a collected pain body from your environment that you life in, your nation perhaps. The truth is any pain you are creating for yourself right now and any pain that you've had in the past still lives in your body and mind. Let's discuss this pain body we all have and how to stop creating a larger pain body and allowing your body to heal from past pain.

Our pain body wants to thrive, live and survive just as our physical body does. It can only live on if you unconsciously bring it forth in your present moment. As a whole, the human race, all of humanity must learn to have body awareness. By having body awareness we are able to remain in the now, the present moment which will set us free from the imprisonment we often unconsciously keep ourselves in. By just being aware of your pain body each time it arises within your physical body you will be able to strengthen your immune system and the body has a boosted ability to heal itself.

Eckhart Tolle, an astonishing spiritual teacher, which Oprah Winfrey has said he is a great prophet of our present day, said this amazing statement about our pain body "All inner resistance is experienced as NEGATIVITY in one form or another. ALL NEGATIVITY is resistance. In this context, the two words are almost synonymous. Negativity ranges from irritation or impatience to fierce anger, from a depressed mood or sullen resentment to SUICIDAL despair. Sometimes the resistance triggers the emotional pain body, in which case even a minor situation may produce intense negativity, such as anger, depression or deep grief." This wise youthful profit of our times is teaching about this pain body to the collective unconsciousness in our world. What he means plainly put is that when we are in a NEGATIVE mindset, we bring on sickness, depression and suicidal tendencies more easily. Letting negative thoughts flow to you, in you and through you is the COMPLETE OPPOSITE of allowing what God would want for your life. In allowing this negativity we ultimately resist any GOOD that wants to flow into us instead.

On this earth you are a drop of water in the ocean of unconsciousness. What you think and put out into the universe really does affect our whole world on the level of thought knowing you are a part of something larger and much greater than your own self. We are one in this world. Rumi, one of my personal favorite personal spiritual leaders of the past. He was said to be a Sufi mystic, a Muslim poet, a theologian. He taught about our universe being as one and said "WE ARE ONE, everything in the universe is within you, ask all from yourself." Rumi guided many people to gain enlightenment like our present day Eckhart Tolle has. Rumi states "Let your heart's light guide your to my house. Let your heart's light show you that we are one." And other quotes from this great poet that like "Inside the great mystery that is, we really doesn't own anything. What is this competition we feel then? Before we go, one at a time, through the same gate?" "Go find yourself so you can find me." "Why struggle to open a door between us when the whole wall is an illusion." He taught about our whole earth being one. The truth is you are but a small drop in the unconscious body of this planet.

These small steps will help you identify your pain body:

- Realize what the situation that elicited your pain body is. (This may be very small)
- Bring your conscious awareness to this pain inside your body ascending
- Feel what your emotion is as it ascends and recognize that it is your pain body
- Shine the light of consciousness on this pain (Know it does not control you)
- Hold it there where it ascends from just being present in the moment

How Your Pain Body Manifest Itself Inside You
Instead of fighting your pain body, watch it silently then let it go away on it's own

Are you aware that you have a pain body? Do you understand that this pain body inside your physical body does not get along with self-awareness, you knowing you? So, in knowing about your pain body and watching it from a conscious level as it arises be fully present when this pain body starts to flare up. Deeply know that you are not this pain body, it is separate from your NEGATIVE self-talk you have. Start to question your pain body as you become aware of its presence inside your mind. Never engage with a tug of war between your conscious state of seeing your pain body, just allow it to be and watch it. Just knowing your pain body is there will make it disappear like smoke clearing out of room on its own.

Our pain body in its hunger or starvation comes to the surface to feast on pain. This monster pain body that we all have inside will create physical pain and illness in your body by allowing it to feast. It manifest as headaches, back pain, neck pain, fibromyalgia, high blood pressure, heart disease, autoimmune disorders, lupus, rheumatoid arthritis, IBS, MVP, heart palpitations and so on. This has been scientifically proven and is taught that there is a link between how you are feeling and your physical state of health.

With this new in depth understanding of knowing we are made of matter which is packed molecules made out of atoms and knowing that every cell in our body has energy inside we know that each cell is like its own self-powered microprocessor. Your cells are vibrating at the frequency of your emotions that are only coming from your thoughts. By becoming in the present moment allowing yourself to see that there is a pain body that emerges inside you to feast you can boost your immune system and heal.

Our bodies cells feast on the outside senses like seeing an ocean, hearing singing birds, tasting the best cupcake in the world, feeling a warm hand touch your back and smelling grandmas apple pie in the oven. More so though, our body's cells feast off of our emotions like anger, resentment, joy, peace, harmony, love, connectedness and hate. This has been studied in the link between what is going on inside of us and what is going on physically with us. It is the unseen facilities in our life that have the most profound impact on our wellbeing. **Abraham Lincoln** knew this when he said "To believe in the things you can see and touch is no belief at all, but to believe in the unseen is a triumph and a blessing."

We Are From A Place Of Love
Forgive them because they don't know what they are doing.

Inside all of us there is an invisible intelligence that drives all of our lives. This intelligence is what drives your most inner desires. It allows your heart to beat freely, our hair to grow and it is the one force that supports all of life anywhere on this planet. To connect to this invisible intelligence, this life giving spirit you must disconnect the consciousness you have of your body.

The light inside is our true essence. We have to become detached from our personalities in order to allow this truth to unveil itself. What you think you are, you are not. In nature everything has an animating force which is unseen behind it. Do you agree? That force is why we have life and without that force life as we know it becomes death as we know it in the physical sense. The doer is unseen that keeps our planets in alignment or that pushes the waves on to shore. Even though we know this unseen force is there, this life giving force, rarely to we take a moment to sit and think about this unseen or invisible intelligence.

Our infants and toddlers often are in this disconnected state until the consciousness of their minds are able to develop. They ate the ones that know the most about God because they have recently been wrapped in the arms of this Divine unseen intelligence, God. "Our birth is but a sleep and a forgetting, not in entire forgetfulness and not in utter nakedness, but trailing clouds of glory do we come" said a famous British poet William Wordsworth. Many stories have been told about small toddlers that express what they remembered before they came to earth. The child prodigy **Akiane Kramarik** is a clear example of this.

When Akiane (which means ocean) was born, she was born into a family of atheist. Neither her father nor mother express any religious belief at all in their home. She was kept away from pre-school and home schooled instead. When she was only 4 years old she started painting astonishing pieces of art that were very spiritual in nature. She told her parents she had "visions" and would paint them as if she was an aged professor teaching art to the finest of art students on earth by the age of 8 years old. She is famous for many of her paintings that are biblical, one best known painting is the one titled "Prince of Peace." This painting was analyzed by the best of the best historians and it is said to be exactly what Jesus would have looked like here on earth. She was only 8 and came from parents that did not share this belief with her. Where did this come from? The Shroud of Turin and her painting resemble each other. This little girl is now in her twenties and states "I don't belong to any denomination or religion, I just belong to God." She says "I am self-taught. In other words, God is my teacher." Her poems are just as touching as her art. "For all eternity I will be gardens with perfect flowers, remembering and missing fallen petals of a fallen world."

She is only one story of a child being able to tell about the place they were before they came to this earth. So many stories about the before life told and about the afterlife told. It blows my mind to think that so many people are walking around unattached to this knowledge. The truth is we all have a light inside, we all can emanate love and it gives us a glow. This love we hold lets our bodies' resonate at a higher frequency and allows a light to come from us in any given situation. The eyes are the window to the soul and when you see a person with this understanding inside look into their eyes, you can see it through their windows.

Send Love To The People That Have Hurt You In The Past
Forgiveness for your own peace, Free YOURSELF

Think about the one person in your life that has given you the most heartache. Instead of holding on to that heartache let it go so that you can free yourself. When you are able to forgive truly then there will always be a release that happens inside yourself. Instead of you attaching to that hurt and identifying to it, you free yourself and become the best you that you can be.

Say this to that one person or to the persons that have harmed you on a deep level in the past. Go on and say it out loud right now "I send you love and light, my friend, from my heart to yours-to love you, to protect you, to guide you, to heal you, to cherish you, to comfort you. God bless you, my friend. You are beautiful and you are loved." While you are saying this prayer of love visualize their face. It may seem inconceivable to you but as sure as you ask the invisible force of life inside you, God to guide you, you have surrendered to a higher form of justice. You do not have to like the person but you should acknowledge that God loves that person the same way that he loves you. Just let go of that hurt inside and free yourself by sending the gift of love to them through the universal energy that you have put out.

<u>What Do You Really Want?</u>
Serve others, enjoy your work, be together with family

Learning that there is more to life that the physical ask yourself what is it that you really desire in life. Do materialistic things make who you are? Or is who you are what is unseen? This is one question that I myself have been thinking hard on. While doing research for this book, I have a deeper understanding that yes, who I am is an intelligence, a source of energy, an expression of a higher power and that who I am is really unseen. Because what is now is only from what was and what will be can bring forth an abundance of other outcomes. This means that my state of being is from the thoughts I had in the past and in my future only comes from thoughts that I continue to have or change. Thoughts are unseen but physical manifestations are outcomes of those thoughts but still, that is not who I am. Who I am is a source of energy.

That is mouth full to swallow but in knowing this you will meet your true self. Meeting your true self allows you to be turned on, tuned in, and tapped in to that higher source of life. When you are in this state of being you are living a limitless life. There are no interruptions only scenarios that are there for your own personal growth therefore allowing an overall growth of the human race because we are all connected. **Dr. Wayne Dyer** says "Our connection others infinite has always beckoned us. We have only to move beyond the barriers we have created to a blissful and empowering view of reality." Seeing clearly, having clarity about everything in life and being in alignment with giving and receiving for the continuous flow of energy to come forth.

When you are asking, allowing and having faith that your desires will manifest in life think about what your true intentions for these desires are. Do not focus on outcome but focus on how you serve humanity.

The Power In Writing It Down
I will succeed because I am crazy enough to believe that I can.

You are a creator. God made us all to have an imagination which is what no other animal on this planet possesses except for human beings. Use your imagination like Einstein did to create the life you desire for wellbeing while you are alive. Ask, allow and trust. While you are creating your life start from where you are now and know that where you are now is just that. Know that where you are going is somewhere different that where you are now. Life is a constant state of expansion and creation. There is power in writing something down that you would like to see change in your life.

7 small steps:

1. Know like you know like you know that you can have whatever you want.
2. Become super clear about what your wishes are and what your intentions are.
3. Feel right now how it would feel if you already had it in your hand now.
4. Study it, every day do something that holds that vision close -WRITE IT DOWN.
5. Become more positive in your thought process towards everything in your life now.
6. Trust that it is a process, have faith it will come at the perfect timing for you.
7. Become super detached to how you will be able to make things happen for you.

Trust that you are a creator of your life and that there is a higher power that moves to you, through you and out of you. Clarity is a key to being able to create a vision of what you want. Make that decision right now. What do you want? Just make a decision. It is hard sometimes to truly be honest with yourself about what you want. Get clear with yourself and connect with your true inner being to get clarity. Thoughts create emotion so let your imagination take you to a place that you can feel how it feels to already have your desires now. Feel how it feels walking around knowing you have that amount of money in the bank or that new car you desire. Do the work and study ways that raise your vibration. Make a circle of focus or a goal card and look at it every day. Write down your goals right now! Write down what you want to happen in three months from now, in a year from now, in five years from now and in ten years from now, get really clear on that. Trust that you will be able to get there and that it may take time to do so. Know that the timing will be perfect and let life happen for you. Get really unattached to figuring out how these things will manifest for you, all you really need to know is that they will.

Be On The Outside Of What You Idealize On The Inside
Act as if you already are the person you want to be.

"Strive to be on the outside of what you idealize of the inside" says Bob Procter when he is teaching about how to shift your paradigm. These lessons are not created right now, this knowledge is ancient and these lessons have been buried in our education systems. These lessons are not taught to us while we are small so it takes shifting your whole truth to be able to really understand how this works.

Right now as you are reading this be that person you idealize to be already. The truth is who are you anyway? Remember from reading we come from a place of love that you are not what you are now because that's only a manifestation of your past. For example if you are 200lbs, overweight now, it is from all that junk you feed your body in the past and you can change that when you have wellbeing in life. If you are this person that is overweight and wanting to manifest a new body weight then first in your mind visualize that you already are that body weight and walk the walk that you already lost the weight you needed to. So, in any given idealization this is the case. Do you want to have more money in the bank? Well believe you already do and that it is coming, walk as if you know you've got it and you will have it.

How Is Your Attitude Effecting Your Results?
Self-talk and say YES I CAN

We are all human. Right? I know you have bad days and I have them too. It's OK to just be human and not get things right sometimes. It is when you figure out that having the attitude of persistence in life is what will get you to your goals in life. This is nothing new, I'm not saying this for the first time. Some of the most successful people we know have this attitude though. Think about it....Michael Jackson, The King of Pop, had this persistence attitude. He never gave up to climb as high as he did as far as fame. Yes, but he was human, and I'm sure he had some really bad days, well....we all know he did.

Think about it really, who else would be on this list? Here, let me name just a few. Napoleon Hill, Eckhart Tolle, Ester Hicks, Tony Robbins, Albert Einstein, Lao Tzu, Buddha, Jesus, Bob Proctor, Oprah Winfrey, Dr. Wayne Dyer, Joel Osteen, Dr. Elizabeth Blackburn, Dr. Joseph Murphy, Jim Carry, Karl Benz, James Allen, Andrew Cardigan, Mel Robbins, Rum Dr. Konstantin Korotkov, Winston Churchill, Louise Hay, Abraham Lincoln, William Wordsworth and Akiane Kramarik to name only a few. Do a few of these names ring a bell? All very famous and successful for their times. What do they know and understand that you may think you understand but not quite yet? I can tell you that their attitude was what got them there. Where does that attitude arise from? A CAN DO ATTITUDE.

Negative Thoughts v/s Positive Thoughts
Are you afraid of change or ready for new experiences?
It's fun to imagine what my future is-
It will never happen, it could happen, it will happen-

"A POSITIVE THINKER SEES THE INVISIBLE, FEELS THE INVISIBLE, FEELS THE INTANGIBLE AND ACHIEVES THE IMPOSSIBLE."- WINSTON CHURCHILL

No more words left to say.

<u>How Dedicated Are You?</u>

Dedication seems to be hard to imagine when our lives are so demanding these days. Dedication to one thing, easy! but dedication pulled in a million different directions is another thing. How are we supposed to give focus to just one thing solely? It is possible if you decide those other things do not need the same dedication because they always do. It's a juggling act. Some of us are really going to create a zombie apocalypse one day because we walk around like zombies now. Like zombies or robots we spend our days doing the same routines over and over. The truth is, dedication takes being very flexible. Nothing will work without bending. Lets say "The Law of FLEXABILITY" – just came up with that at this very moment.

What else is flexible in your life? Water? It's no wonder why The Bible, The Tao or any other spiritual book makes so many references to water. Jesus said "Those who drink the water I will give them will never be thirsty again but the water I give them will be a well of water springing up to eternal life." John 4: 13-14

Water? Flexible? Yes lets let water be our teacher.

Water is a never ending constant resistance force in nature. Teacher water can show us some laws of the universe. It is an amazing wonderful creation from God. Let it teach you how bending can create enormous ruts. Water can cut through clay sharper than enough when it's a body of water. The water's edge is never sharp there's a constant bending that takes place. Water is very symbolic.

Verse 8: Flow like Water
"True goodness Is like water.
Water's good for everything.
It doesn't compete.

It goes right to the low loathsome places,
And so finds the way.

For a house,
The good thing is level ground.

In thinking, Depth is good.
The good of giving in magnanimity,
Of speaking, honestly,
Of government, order.
The good of work is skill.
And of action, timing.

No competition,
So no blame."
Tao Te Ching

Is Your Life Worth It?
*"Life isn't worth living, unless it is lived for
someone else." Albert Einstein
-Serve others for yourself-*

You are a spiritual being, you are intellectual and you are a
physical being. With the three of these important aspects to your
life you will see a constant growth in your life, your life will be
forever expanding. The first step to having a major life changing
manifestation occur in your life is to find out what exactly is your
priority of desires. Basically put, what your focus on will grow
stronger in life. What do you put your focus on? Is taking the
time to analyze this thought important to you? Are there things
you would like for your life that you do not have in this present
moment? Know that without a doubt- you will have it in a future
moment but you must know that life is worth it to have that faith in
mind.

In our society, we've got it all wrong. I am just figuring this
out as I study these principles of these very successful people of
today and of the past. Society tells us we must go to work to make
money. The truth is we shouldn't go to work to make money, we
should be going because it makes us feel good to be a service
for others. The richest of rich people that are living today have
multiple sources of income and are rarely living a day to day
schedule that requires them to clock in and clock out. They've
figured out that being a service to others never requires them to
do that. They make money while they are asleep from multiple

sources of income. Instead of trading there time for money, they have multiple sources of money that is constantly flowing to them. Also, they have time for vacations and time to spend with their families. This concept is mind blowing when you start to actually think about it.

This universe is a forever expanding universe. It is said to be ten billion light years in diameter and contains innumerable Galaxies. Life, are we the only life in this universe that is ten billion light years in diameters with other galaxies? If so, wouldn't you'd say life is rare or life is a one in a tens of billions and forever expanding numbers of length in ratios of one to whatever that number is? And even if we are not the only life in our universe, it'd still be rare according to the numbers of planets that do not hold life on them to those that could. Questions to ask yourself and think about.

Signs And How They Are Guiding You
Impulses & Intuition

There are two aspects of this topic. The physical and the non-physical. Which one do you think is more important? It is always and forever will be the unseen. What we hold inside our bodies, our impulses and our intuition. Let your feelings be your guide. Have you ever been trying to make a decision and you've asked God to show you a sign? "Just show me a sign!" Well I am telling you that if you get quite and quit looking for the answers outside of yourself then you will always have the guidance you need. We are programmed to look from things outside out ourselves to give us belief. Believe in yourself is all that it takes to have confidence and guidance though. Pay attention to HOW YOU FEEL! How are you feeling?

Do you like the feeling of clarity? Can you feel when something is shifting? Do you feel inspired to say something? Do you ever get a hunch about something? Do you ever feel inspired to just give someone something? Do you like the feeling of abundance? Do you like the feeling of being alive? Does it feel great to teach? Is it wonderful to create something new? Doesn't it feel like a blessing to be a positive role model? Do you enjoy being an inspiration for others? All of these feelings you are having are the signs from within that are directing your steps in life for growth.

When we go within it is THEN that the physical signs start to appear for confirmation instead of for guidance. Play with this knowledge today. Think about a bluebird, talk about a blue \bird to a friend for a brief moment then let it go. Watch that bluebird cross your path at some point depending on how fast you allow it to show itself. This is so true. We must practice this state of allowing things to flow into our life with no thoughts that carry the vibration of resistance. Did you know that the pretty bluebird is the male? Ask, allow and trust. By not having resistance to anything and just trusting this process things or signs will appear to you due to your own thoughts and vibration you have put out. Rather that bluebird is an actual bluebird that crosses your path or a picture of the bluebird is totally up to your thought process on manifestation.

I could talk about numbers being seen 1111 or 111 or 333 or 444 but those numbers are being seen as a manifestation of your own thoughts and ideas rather than a sign. These numbers will appear to you when you are in alignment with different desires in life. When your awareness or clarity become sharper and you are not having resistance. You are then in the mode of receiving.

Your Spirit Guides

What is a spirit? It is a nonphysical part of you that is the seat of emotions and character, the soul. Also spirit can be a temperament or disposition of mind or outlook when animated. Spirit is described as being the immaterial intelligent or sentient part of person. It is also said to be that you have spirit when you hold a special attitude or frame of mind about something. So, spirit guides are nothing but a certain spirit that arises inside us that we bring forth by raising our vibration to a higher state of being. Our spirit then becomes impulsive and electrical and it is those impulses that are guiding us. Again, we want to look for spirit guides to be something outside of ourselves when we have these spirit guides or this nonphysical part inside all of us. It is not like an actual person comes to us and guides us. We have to get into that alignment state, clarity state, non-resistance state, allowing state and the state of receiving to change our emotions that then raise our vibration and state of being.

"Do you know that your bodies are temples of the Holy Spirit, who is in you, whom you have received from God? You are not your own" 1 Corinthians 6:19

Angles Guarding Us
"Angels at my fingertips." Lorna Byrne

This topic- such a delicate topic as it is, in my research I reached up outside of myself and waited until my emotions lead me to write about this. I felt like out of all the topics in this book, this one is special and needed time to meditate on it for a day or so. Not only that, I questioned my own belief on this. As I start to write it all comes back to me though. During my meditation and research on angles a brilliant thing happened. Lorna Byrne came to me very very very unexpected. I never heard of this woman before ever in my life. She is an Irish author and peace ambassador with an amazing mystical gift. She explains that ever sense as far back as she can remember, even as a baby, she remembers seeing angles. She didn't realize that others were not seeing these beings like she was. Much wiser with age now, she has helped others have some eye opening experiences. Her guardian angles even told her about her books being top sellers as she was a small child before she knew how to write.

The truth is the Earth is a true mysterious place. Religions have divided us and wars have broken out over religions but we were never meant to be on the earth to be divided. It is so hard to not to place humans in a category on earth. That's what we do every single day. You're a Jew, You're a Christian, You're Asian, You're African American, You're an Atheist, You're a Buddhist, You're tall, You're short, You're a blonde, You're a redhead, You're this, you're that but I am this and I am that. We separate ourselves. It's something only consciousness or being enlightened can show you. When you see it, you are opened to knowing that there is just so much we do not understand about our Universe and Angles being present here is not a fictional story, they are real physical beings that are in our world. As Lorna Byrne says "I am not of this world, I am in this world." She says that the Angles taught so much and not being of earth or from earth is one of those things. Her hope is that we can all unite as one and pray together in acceptance of our differences. That would be pretty cool if we could.

Have you ever seen an angel? I have, no kidding. A beautiful angel that stood tall above me, gave me a message and kissed my forehead when I was 18 years old. This angel I saw came to me and gave me a specific message about a situation I was in. I actually took her advice and it was the best decision in the world.

It Is What It Is
Acceptance= control

My apartment flooded 10 days after I just moved in due to a hurricane. I didn't have renters insurance and most of my belongings were ruined. At that time also, I was going through a break up with a guy that I was with for 4 years and I just started a nursing school program. Three major stressors in my life happened all at once. In a month I ended up moving not once, not twice, not three times but four times total meanwhile maintaining a job and full time nursing school. My attitude kept me alive along with all the people in my life that were under me praying for me and offering their assistance. Life happens, we all have stories like this. Being the artist that I am, my first painting was on an old piece of wood from the rubble of the hurricane. On it I painted "It is what it is." That piece of painted wood hangs on my wall and I look at it every day.

The truth is that when something major happens in your life, you cannot change it. You do not have the power to change whatever is. What you do have power over is your attitude. Accept what is and let it be. When that flood happened, I wrote a post about having a clean slate and thanked God for it. I looked at the flood as a symbol for purging for what was better to come in my life. There was so much I needed to let go anyway so, I did. I had a deep understanding that I could have acceptance of what is and by accepting it I did not allow my circumstance have control over me. I had control, I started a new life, a new chapter in life.

Part 3
Making Decisions:
How is personal power put into action?

Going From Point A to Point B

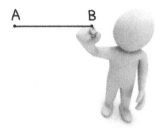

Small details of life give contrast

Contrast is what makes a painting pop. The **contrast** of the corral against the blue and hazy hues of purple and gray to complement each other make that painting is what it is. Without offering contrast to a picture the scene will be **bland and dull**. There is nothing that our mind grabs to and thinks **"WOW"** about. When a painting does have that **"WOW"** factor, it has so many aspects of different contrast that arise from the center of the painting to all four corners of that piece of art. It is the contrast that you offer in life that will also make your life have that "WOW" factor. When we want to go from the point where we are now in life (A) to another point in life (B) then we must allow for contrast to take place in life. Get out of those daily boring routines that are not offering contrast and trust that you will get there. Contrast offers colorful balance to your painting of life.

When you call an Uber driver from your iPhone app to come pick you up when you need a ride, you trust that Uber driver will come for you. You know you have to get to that destination and you have no doubt at all that you can find some way or another to get yourself there. You may not know all the details like what that Uber driver looks like, his name, the route you will take or the type of car he is driving. What you do know is that you are getting in that car (point A) and it will take you to your destination (point B). You never doubt that, you never offer resistance about that so, you get there. All the little details in-between the point from where you were picked up at (point A) to where you were dropped off (point B) were unknown. That's how our Universe works, use this example for a physical manifestation of knowing this same exact concept works in your life in nonphysical ways as well when you want to make a major change. You may not know how you will get there but it's the knowing aspect of the going aspect that will get you there. You may not know how you're going to reach that goal but just by not having resistance to the idea that you will reach that goal and trusting that you will reach it, you will reach it one way or another.

Going anywhere takes having a true sense of trust in knowing you will get there sooner or later. If at any time you doubt that due to the contrast life offers **NEVER QUIT** knowing you will get there. Do not do a "U TURN" in the road that you are on and go back to your same point, your point A. Keep going on until you get to point B and **NEVER EVER DOUBT** that you will get there just because you may not see the outcome so fast. Some roads take longer to travel, just know where you are going (clarity) and get there without turning around even if you have to take some pit stops (allowing).

Our universe gives us physical examples to unphysical lessons, just open your eyes to see them.

There are seven pairs of CONTRAST that are recorded in the life of man: (this comes from ancient knowledge 2nd century

BCE book called **Sefer Yetzirah** (means the book of creation that a Hebrew lore said was **written by Adam from Adam and Eve**) ...here comes the number "7" again....AND YES, I said Adam from the book of Genesis in the Bible was said to have written a book and this comes from it.

1. **Life and death**
2. **Peace and strife**
3. **Wisdom and folly**
4. **Wealth and poverty**
5. **Beauty and ugliness**
6. **Fertility and sterility**
7. **Lordship and servitude**

Find Your Earthly Destiny
Do you believe that you will feel better in the having of it?

If there is something that you really want to know, become the teacher. Study it until you can teach it. Find vibrational alignment with who you really are. Your desire is your path toward your destiny. Destiny is lining up with who you really are, your fun, your definition and your empowerment. More experience **is not needed** to **be who you really are**. Your destiny is to be in charge of your experience. If there is a gap in-between your state of being now and your state of being that is limitless, close that gap by knowing you are responsible for coming into full alignment with who you are, your wholeness. We are **spiritual** beings, we are **intellectual** beings and we are **physical** beings. Mind, body and soul is being whole. Mind, body and soul for your wellbeing.

When we talk about destiny we often think it is that one thing in life that will bring us to true happiness. The word DESTINY even gives you a feeling of goodness that rushes through your veins just saying the word. When we place the value higher on destiny being in our future and live in the future then we are not being grateful for what we have in the now. Being in the now, being present is so important and having gratitude for all you have now is the key to getting our desires in life. We have to be in a vibrational match to our desires to get our desires. In not feeling good now, you only bring forth more of not feeling good. Re-frame your thoughts to a place of gratefulness and thankfulness. Be at peace with your present situation knowing that you will have your desires unfold soon. Our desires are our path to our destiny in life. Really do what makes you feel good now, do not worry about the outcomes. Know that now is what it is, accept what is, give appreciation for what is, and put love into the universe. What is to come will be even greater when you do that.

Perceive & Achieve
See yourself already in possession of your goal-

Write down a descriptive note to yourself in order to see changes take place in your life. Place a copy of your note where you can look at it multiple times a day. Autosuggestion will change your subconscious thoughts and steer them in the direction of your desires. Use your imagination! Man can create anything that he or she can imagine. Where is your self-motivation also? What is your attitude? You may have to check yourself at times. As you write yourself this note know that you may need to change it from time to time. Do not concern yourself with limitations. You will rise above your limitations because things are always working out for you.

When I discovered this lesson a few months ago, I wrote a bill to myself. What I owe myself. We are always receiving bills in the mail so, I decided I did owe myself a few things instead of owing anyone else anything. I wrote at top- "Bill to myself" – "What I owe myself"- Then I listed my desires and goals on that bill. I was specific with a handful of important desires I wanted to manifest in the next quarter of the year and one thing I wanted to achieve by the end of the year. Since 1 month has past I have already achieved one of those main goals! It happened so quickly!

Get really clear about what it is you desire. Make a plan on how your goals or desires will be achieved. You cannot ever get something for nothing, it's a law of the universe. Have courage, self-control, be decisive, do more than what you are paid for, be responsible, have willpower, make a positive habit, use persistence and use your imagination. Decision or being decisive is so important. We must learn how to actually make a decision promptly. Knowing you may change your mind on decision and then know you must change it slowly. For example, make a decision you want to make X amount of money in a year but if you change your mind and want to make more or less then change your mind slowly on that. Earl Nightingale and Napoleon Hill teaches this lesson in books about success. This lesson is nothing knew past down from generations of men. So many people have not heard of this because they are stuck sitting in front of a television be hypnotized by junk food television. Napoleon Hill stresses that you will make money while you sleep it you understand this concept well.

Write a bill to yourself

Bill to Self:	Quarter _____ Year_____
Month 1	• _____ • _____
Month 2	• _____ • _____
Month 3	• _____ • _____
For the Year: I owe myself:	• _____ • _____ • _____

What you can have definite perception about you
will be able to bring about in your life.
Everything starts with an impulse of a thought.

Hold that mental picture in your mind,
Hold the desire in your heart,
You will see it in your hands.

Choose Your Purpose and Attain It
What is your intention?

Ask yourself "what is really important to me in this situation?"
"Who is it that will benefit from this?" Seek that clarity in your
desires. Also, get emotional about it! What do you want to feel?
Generate how you want to feel. Get really clear on your visions for
yourself and when that vision is clear get super emotional about it.
Say to yourself "I must do well." Say to yourself "I am a person that
cares about high standards." See yourself as a high performer.
Set that self-image for yourself as being a high performer. Drive,
purpose and urgency will drive you towards attain anything in your
life. Do you know what next habits to start? Do you have another
level of life that you can live?

It Does Not Matter Where You Are Now
Use the "Thought Experiment"

When we gain weight, we gain it over time right? So say you
are 120lbs right now. If you'd eat a dozen donuts every day for a
few months, you'd put some pounds on. So what your body weight
is right now is only a manifestation of what your thought process
lead you to eat in your past. So, what are you are growing in your
mind right now with your thoughts, will bring the fruit of those
thoughts. We are what we think. Action is the blossom of thoughts
and joy or suffering is its fruits.

This is a simple matter of cause and effect. The effect of
cherished associations of your imaginary ideas will cause a
manifestation to be brought about in life. Of all the beautiful truths
of life, this one is true. Man is the master of thought, the maker
and shaper of destiny. Human beings hold the key to their own
destination. Only by searching and mining are precious gems and
gold found. We must learn how to dig deep and do some mining

in our own thoughts. Albert Einstein understood this concept because he constantly came up with some life changing questions he asked himself. He actually had a scientific process he called "thought experiments."

Einstein used these thoughts to imagine some life changing discoveries:
- Imagine you are chasing a beam of light- "Special Theory of Relativity"-
- Imagine you're are standing on a train- A "cornerstone in "Special Theory of Relativity"-
- Imagine you have a twin in a rocket ship-"Light clock thought-passage of time"-
- Imagine you're standing in a box- "General Theory of Relativity"-
- Imagine you're tossing a two-sided coin- "Quantum Entanglement"-

The Power Of Guiding Your Mind Into Direction

"The light of the body is the eye; if therefore thine eye be single, thy whole body shall be full of light. But if thine eye be evil, thy whole body shall be full of darkness. If therefore the light that is in thee be darkness, how great is that darkness!" Matthew 6:22-23

Bioelectromagnetics- The Human Aura
&
The Pineal Gland

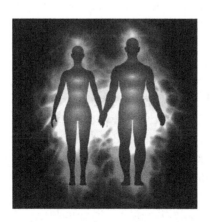

What is Bioelectromganetics?
What is the human aura made of?
What is an Arc? Electrical arcing?
How does the pineal gland effect our aura?
Heart & Brain Communications

These are the questions I asked myself when I started to learn that we have the power to guide our minds to have the abundance in life that we all desire. Something deep inside me wanted to know the answers to these questions because I knew from a small child that we are more than just flesh. We have a spiritual side that taps into emotions that cause us to take a turn in life, that help to guide our thoughts into a clearer direction.

Bioelectromganetics is the study of the interaction between electromagnetic fields and biological entities. The study of electro fields produced by living cells, tissues or organisms even including bacteria, our stars, our planets, humans, animals, the chair you're sitting in and so forth. Dumbed way down, the easy way to put this into understanding is that every single thing created in this universe has a vibration and an electromagnetic field. This filed, this bioelectromagnetic field we all have extends 4-5 feet in a healthy body but is less than that from a person that is unhealthy. The level of health a person is in has a direct effect of how our aura is portrayed out into the universe. Because matter is not solid, it is composed up of mainly empty space (like I talked about in Part 1 of this book) and this empty space holds electrical currents that resonates out our vibration. This may sound "crazy" or fictional information but the truth is we do have auras and what they are made up is pure energy. Where does our energy originate from? Our emotions.

Our hearts have been studied and it has been proven scientifically that our hearts create the largest electromagnetic fields out of the entire body. How does the heart and brain communicate with each other? How does it affect our consciousness and our perceptions? When we are feeling positive emotions, the heart beats out a certain message. By learning to shift our emotions, it changes the magnetic fields radiated by the heart and it effects the others around us. By learning that our hearts and our minds are connected and work as one entity we can shift our experiences in life. Our heart has an intuitive intelligence. There has been dedicated research in the scientific community in studying this link between the two. There is ongoing research in global coherence in the Earth's electromagnetic fields and the collective consciousness. Every SINGLE THING in the universe has an aura! EVERTHING, which is NOTHING BUT ENERGY, connects with everything in the universe.

Doc Childre is an imaginative scientist that dedicates his life in research to understand the hearts intelligence he says "Heartmath research confirms our intuitive understanding of the heart with solid science and explains how the electromagnetic field radiating from the heart can affect those around us." He also said "What you put out comes back. The more you sincerely appreciate life from the heart, the more the magnetic energy of appreciation attracts fulfilling life experiences to you, both personally and professionally. Learning how to appreciate more consistently offers many benefits and applications. Appreciation is an easy heart frequency to activate and it can help your perspectives quickly. Learning how to appreciate both pleasant and even seemingly unpleasant experiences is a key to increased fulfillment." **Doc Childre**

How are our electromagnetic fields connected with our pineal gland? Our pineal gland is that small gland that looks similar to a pinecone shape in the center of our brains. It is the only part of the brain that is not divided into two separate parts yet it links all the parts of the brains together. Bathed in the highly charged CSF (cerebrospinal fluid) and having more blood flow per cubic volume than any other organ in our body, the pineal gland has the highest concentration of energy in our body! In addition to that, it is the main source of melatonin secreted into our bloodstreams. It also secrete other consciousness enhancing neurochemical in our bodies like DMT and serotonin. This small gland is known as the "third eye" and the "seat of the human soul." The pineal gland hold some interesting abilities that ancient cultures even knew about. Long before modern day science the ancient cultures (the Egyptians) spoke of the "third eye" and drew it the same as the how our pineal gland looks in our brain, and it looks like an eye. How did they know it contains photo receptors? This knowledge is nothing new what I am talking about here. This has been understood and known for years long before modern day technologies.

Brain scans indicate that the pineal gland activity increases with meditation. It is also believed that we can tune this gland to certain frequencies and connect with the universal frequencies becoming oneness with everything in the universe. By activating the pineal gland we expand our consciousness and raise our vibration which in turn increases our human body's aura. How do we open that eye so that our bodies have this light that was talked about in the Bible? There is much to be said about this topic. There have been various ways to help our pineal glands to open. Being able to focus (visualize) and to meditate are at the top of these. To guide our minds into any direction we must become conscious and utilize the power of our pineal glands. God made our minds, our bodies and our souls why not learn how to fully use our brain power?

An arc is defined as a continuous passage of electrical current between two or more separated carbon or other electrodes. OUR BRAINS HAVE THIS ELECTRICAL ARC!!!! Nerve impulses in the body are triggered across our synaptic clefts which are electrical impulses. In the brain the impulses arc from one receptor to the other. When we engage in meditation we receive light energy through the pineal gland which then cause Arcs of electricity. The covenant is the electrical light message flowing to us from a higher state of thinking that keeps us in harmony with the universal greater power. Where have you heard this work "Acr" before? Arc-Ark.... Ark of the Covenant? Noah's Ark? Archangels? These are the types of questions I think about or have "thought experiments" about.

Success Begins With A Clear Picture in Your Mind's Eye
Divine Consciousness is everything
Sacred geometry & the golden ratio

Do you know what this symbol is? It's a symbol of manifestation. The "SRI YANTRA" is a 12,000 year old.... YES!! 12,000 YEAR OLD symbol used as a tool for obtaining consciousness that leads to the awareness of what we really want in life and shines light so our mind's eye can see that our universe lives in a state of divine consciousness. The word "SRI YANTRA" means "holy instrument" and is also known as the "holy wheel." In this holy instrument there is the sacred geometrical golden ratio which we all should be aware of. The golden ratio is found in shells, our universal galaxy swirl, sunflowers, DNA, snails, plants and I could go on and on so you'd get my point. It is seen in anything of beauty on this earth. Golden proportion is seen in our faces and our bodies (which is 1.618) based on the Fibonacci sequence. Everything starts as a tiny speck and expands into proportions of 1.618 from a microscopic level. **Pythagoras**, one famous mathematician also said the golden ratio was the blue print of all creation.

In the center of this symbol there is a tiny speck and this symbol is based from this sacred golden ratio. Used with meditation it helps us to focus on spiritual benefits for wellbeing in our lives. Using this symbol to concentrate on while clearing our minds to concentrate of clarity of our lives will enhance the feeling of oneness within ourselves. This symbol is also used to represent the union of the divine masculine and feminine. The Sri Yantra is also said to look strikingly similar to the Star of David.

Staring at the center dot or "bindu" of the symbol is proven to create changes in our brains!!! Proven scientifically while doing brain scans it shows an increase in our Pineal gland. What does our pineal gland do? Some very amazing things as mentioned previously. Our pineal gland is our "third eye" of our bodies that even has **photo receptors** located on it. When we allow ourselves to step out of what we are now programmed in how we think into asking ourselves some important eye opening questions is when we start to really become aware of what we desire in life. The funny thing is, at this point, you start to realize what is important and it is feeling good. When we allow ourselves to just feel good our vibration rises and we bring to us anything our world desires because we will understand in having that physical manifestation become a materialist physical entity in our reality has nothing to do with our state of life. Our state of life is now raised to a higher state which you pull in an infinite source of love and abundance that flows like a river through our vessels that we call our bodies.

It will not hurt to try looking at this symbol and allowing your mind to focus on the center. Once you do this you may notice that the triangles shift as your consciousness deepens. Think about building your foundations for a richer life.

- Imagine that your body rest at the center of the squares
- 4 doors to the external world around you
- The top door is North
- The bottom door is South
- Then on the two sides East and West
- Feel your breath from entering your body from the North then South then East then West
- Focus on your breathing deeply in and then out
- These portals are the four portals to the universe
- Allow your breathing to center you
- Enter an area that you create in your mind that is a heavenly place, visualize this place

- As you come here, take it all in by noticing you the colors around you
- Your mind is what can keep you positive and happy
- Notice what kind of sounds you hear in your sanctuary of peace

Practicing visualization and meditation with deep breathing really does allow our minds to open up to allowing our true desires and becoming at one with ourselves. See yourself having the success in life that makes you feel amazing from the deepest place in your heart. Allow your hearts frequency to raise your vibration so that you call into your world what it is that you truly desire. With God, the unseen enormous power of our universe, we can connect consciously with everyone to raise a divine universal consciousness.

Clarity Can Be Achieved
KNOW THE FACTS
Fluoride a toxic poison= calcification of our third eye pineal gland
-Prozac is Fluoride-

There is so much to be said about the pineal gland and it's abilities that it gives us as human beings. Some may argue the truths behind the abilities that our pineal glands give us. Research has been done over and over again with astonishing truthful reports of proof though. Some men have made millions claiming how to teach others to use there pineal gland and have the "third eye awakening." The third eye is the root to seeds planted and is where our will power is deeply rooted as well.

In America we have fluoride added to our water sources. What is fluoride? Do you know what fluoride is? It's actually a poison! Do you know when they started to add it to our water systems? Do you know that is causes CALCIFICATION of our pineal glands? Do you know fluoride is found to be directly deposited in our pineal glands, our third eye, our seat of our souls, and our seed of will power and cause it to harden shown over and over again on brain scans? This is not fiction. I am not pushing my values here at all, I am simple shining a light on a subject that needs to be known.

Because the pineal gland is in the center of the brain, it is the only gland of the brain that does not have two divided half's and it does not have the blood brain barrier like the rest of our brain does. It has the highest source of blood circulation flowing through it as well. Anything we put in our bodies gets broken down and is distributed through our circulatory systems. It just so happens that fluoride can't be filtered out of the pineal gland and it hardens it or calcifies it. When it is calcified, we can't have a deep third eye awakening. Does our government know about this? Sounds kind of "out there" doesn't it? The facts are the facts though. What does this mean? This means that your pineal gland could have calcifications on it if you use fluoride treated water, drink it and brush your teeth with it. What about cavities and dental hygiene? What about all the other countries that do not add fluoride to their water? Many European countries have banned fluoride including: Austria, Belgium, Finland, France, Germany, Hungary, Luxembourg, Netherlands, Northern Ireland, Norway, Sweden, Switzerland, Scotland, Iceland and Italy.

Interesting facts about fluoride: I'm just saying.......look for yourself:

- **Active ingredient in RAT POISON**
- **Active ingredient in PROZAC- Fluoxetine (which is water, nitrogen, oxygen, carbon & fluoride** (18.5% of Prozac is straight fluoride)
- Fluoride has **never been approved by FDA**
- Most countries do not fluoride their water
- Fluoride effects may tissues of our ENTIRE body
- The counties using fluorinated water do not have less tooth decay
- **Fluoride is the KEY COMPONET of the atom bomb!!!**
- Fluoride is a TOXIC byproduct of ALUMINUM
- IT is illegal to dump fluoride into our lakes and waters
- Added to our water systems in the 1940's
- Fluoride causes early puberty in girls

It is said that Hitler put fluoride in water at concentration camps to induce prisoners into a zombie like state. There is so much controversy surrounding this topic. Just because we have been doing this addition of fluoride to our water systems for over 60 years now, does it make it right? 60 years ago what else was different? How has our world changed in 60 years? Have we gained huge technologies since then? Yes! Do your research and see what you think. **Does it disturb you to know that the main active ingredient in Prozac is fluoride?** Why have you not questioned this before? That is exactly what I am asking myself now. What!!!!????

To be able to have a clear visualization of our future we need our pineal glands to be in full function. The eye on top of the pyramid of the dollar bill in the US ring a bell? Why put this ONE EYE on the pyramid of our money? DO the two have a link? I think so. Understanding this topic may have stirred some unwanted emotions up, do not fear it. There is a time and place for our world to be opened to changes that are much needed. There are things we can do to decalcify our pineal glands though so that we are able to gain clarity of our futures. Our will, our soul, our visualization and God is said to be linked to the function our pineal glands. This special gland deep seated inside our brains holds special powers and we have to learn this information to be able to enter a state of wellbeing of life.

Being A Leader

A leader, a role model, someone you look up to, someone that collaborates with all aspects of a company, a strong individual, a teacher, a mentor, a person that gives guidance and a person that trust others to get the job done. Think about the leader in your company. What does she or does he do outside of what you do? If you are the leader, what aspects of yourself can you say inspires others? Do you take initiative and make some calls on important issues? What does that involve? Making a decision!

To be able to make decisions is a habit we all must learn to have rather or not we are a leader of a company or not. Truth of the matter is we are the leader of our life, so we ALL are leaders. Human beings hold the power within ourselves for creation which comes from imagination but without being able to be clear with a decision nothing will ever happen. Before the US decided to fly a rocket to the Moon a decision was made to do so. President Kennedy knew that making that decision would be a tough one to accomplish but he made that decision anyway. Before you launch your rockets of desires you must learn to make clear decisions.

Guilt and Negative Emotions

When you start to apply some of the lessons talked about in this book and you start to achieve your goals and dreams sometimes you may experience a wave of guilt for having more than others. It is sad to see a single mother with three children riding in a beat up car down the road with a headlight out. Apart of my heart goes out to that mother and then guilt sinks in. I start to think why she has to go through that when I am having such a different reality than she does. We have to understand that we are the ones in control of our own lives though. You made the decision to read this book, you brought into your life the knowledge of creating your own life outcomes, you have done the work, you have studied hard so do not allow yourself to get sucked down with negative guilt emotions.

We know that emotions create our vibrational frequency that goes out into the universe and we know that we have to become aware of them so that no wrong message is sent out. Instead of focusing your thoughts on what they do not have focus them on what they do have and send a gift of loving thoughts towards them. They are the only ones that can open their own world for expansion along with the higher power in our universe.

Do not allow negativity to creep up on you when you've achieved some amazing things and others in your life are not doing so well. We have to know without any doubt that they do have the will power to change their reality just as we did or will be doing. Caring about what other people think is the link to your guilty emotions. When we allow the thoughts of what others think about us we become their prisoner. Lao Tzu- "Care about what other people think and you will always be their prisoner." So reintroduce yourself to your own guidance systems when you start to go down that guilt rabbit hole.

You do want to bring love into your life in all aspects of life, that emotion that attaches to love right? That feeling you get when you love something puts yourself in a higher vibration and feeling great! Instead of perceiving that others are passing any judgments on you, perceive that that you are only putting out those loving blessings and know that those always without any doubt will come back to you in one form or another. Focus on being in the present. Line up with the truth of any situation, stand in your knowing of what you know!!! Stand up with the goodness that your inner self knows that you are!!!! Shine your light and do not take on judgment on you!! Tuned in, tapped in and turned on to that flow of love in your life.

The Ego- How It Effects Decisions
It is not about being right or wrong
Failure is not failure
No wrong paths

When making a decision about anything we often seek advice of others before that decision is made. Any great leader will tell you that having their EGO in charge of making decisions will destroy a team player attitude. When problems arise we must always see them as an opportunity and seek assistance with others to do so. Everybody offers some type of special positivity to any give situation and others can offer feedback that will be constructive. Instead of worrying about the world sees you as what others think, you go deeper inside you start to understand that making a decision is not being about the one having the power. Instead use your value system for decision making and then there is always a better outcome.

The freedom to choose and make decisions is an amazing gift we have. Every choice we make is should be based off of the emotions we feel. Get real with yourself about who you are and align with that of who you know is who the best you that you can be. When you do this then any decision can be made with full blown confidence knowing that any decision is not ever going to be wrong anyway. There really are not any mistakes really. When you do not know that we come from a bigger than us power, God, and when you are in your small way of thinking you get confused about who you are. It is when you connect with the knowledge that we are really are ONE and get centered you know that there is a greater destiny for your life anyway. Everything leads to the same path really. You get as much from any loss than you do from any gain when you think about it.

Failure is a huge fear for many people in life. It was for me at some many points in life but when I started to understand that failure really is not failure then I started to explore a different world beyond what I knew as my current reality. I took a risk and was not afraid. At first I had blind faith but the longer I studied some major basic principles in life then more I knew that the universe always had my back. I knew everything will always work out for me no matter what and I do believe that whole heartedly.

Oprah Winfrey holds an interview at a College and is asked about decisions and failure. She talks about how we look at failures in life as such catastrophes but actually when or if you do fail look at it as just pointing you in the right direction instead. Your losses are really only there to WAKE YOU UP! Your life is so much bigger than any ONE decision. Relax and know it really will BE OK!!!! When you are not at ease with yourself that is when you know you must not be going in the right direction. Pay attention to your emotions, get centered, and think to yourself "what is the next right move?" We know we are not defined by what anyone else says that failure was for us because you know that you have just been directed into another direction. Decisions are important and are needed to move forward in life, we must not fear making mistakes and failing because there really is no such thing.

How Happiness Is A Decision

"I'M GOING TO BE HAPPY. I'm going
to SKIP. I'm going to be glad
I'm going to be easy. I'm going to count my blessings.
I'm going to look for REASONS to feel good

*I'm going to dig up POSITIVE things from the past...I'm
going to look for POSITIVE things where I stand.
I'm going to look for POSITIVE in the future...It is
my NATURAL STATE to be a HAPPY person.
It's natural for me to LOVE and to LAUGH.
This is what is most natural to me.
I AM A HAPPY PERSON!" – Abraham Hicks*

Tune in to the higher source of energy that moves to you, in you, through you and then back out of you and just be happy. Feel the feeling of what love feels like to you. When we have things thrown are way seen as speed bumps in the road we can either let the thoughts carry us into a panic mode or get centered and know that we are the ones in control of our emotions by our thinking process. Can anything be dangerous about you feeling happy instead of feeling sad all the time? Yes, we have to go through processes sometimes to accept what reality is but when we get into a wiser way of thinking we process things differently.

Our bodies have a true physical response to a negative state of mind. It is ok to notice you go through this at times but do not let it take you down that same rabbit hole that is has in the past, do not allow the same cycles happen. Notice that your emotions are related to your thoughts and decide instead to just feel good and just feel happy. I think you should be happy today, be happy every day. Yes, you deserve to be happy every day. It becomes a habit when you start to practice it then others start to notice. Why are you so happy? Because I choose to be, there does not have to be a reason.

Try telling people that ask you why you are so happy when they ask that your happiness depends on you and they are off the hook. Then, be happy no matter what is going on. Show them that it is ok to be happy even though the world is spinning fast. This is when you learn a great habit, not letting anyone else hold the responsibility of making you happy or making you the way you feel at all ever. Love others in ways you have never loved them before BECAUSE you have no reason to not love anyone! If nobody is responsible for your emotional state except for you then you have NO EXCUSE anymore to USE ANYONE ever again as an EXCUSE to not feel good. Don't say "I don't feel good because _____ did this or _____ didn't do that." Do not say "_____ makes me so happy because_____ or _____makes me so mad because they did _____." Truth of this is that you feel that way because you have chosen to do so. Yes, its nice when others pay you a compliment or gives you a gift but you have to choose to feel good regardless of what the outside physical world is doing.

Are You Ready To Have Understanding
"You are the only problem you will ever have and you are the only solution." Bob Proctor

"My disclosures lead to the truth; the mind is great and guided by this teaching is able to arrive at some understanding. When the mind has understood all things and found them to be in harmony with what has been expounded by teachings, it is faithful and comes to rest in that beautiful faith." Hermes Trismegistus

More than understanding that there is a higher power in our universe, you must know that the laws of the universe have a key role in creating our outcomes in life. The law of attraction says the more you think of something the more you get of something. DO you really understand this? When you think about how much debt you have all the time the only thing you are doing is creating more of it. So, instead think about ways you can make money more than you think about your lack of it. The more you think about something you will get it. So, because you start to think about ways to make money more often then ideas flow freely to you, that one special idea will come to you by your alignment with the vibrational forces of the universe.

Knowing that there are just more laws than the law of attraction you must have a deep understanding of those laws as well.

1. The Law of Oneness
2. The Law of Vibration
3. The Law of Action
4. The Law of Correspondence

5. The Law of Cause and Affect
6. The Law of Compensation
7. The Law of Attraction
8. The Law of Perpetual of Transmutation of Energy
9. The Law of Relativity
10. The Law of Polarity
11. The Law of Rhythm
12. The Law of Gender

Each one of these Laws of our universe hold the key for balance in our life. This is nothing new I am discussing here. They stem from an accident knowledge called **Hermeticism**. These books now known as Corpus Hermeticism were part of a renaissance of syncretistic and intellectualized pagan thought that took place from 3rd to 7th century AD. In 1614, Isaac Casaubon analyzed the Greek hermetic text and concluded that the books were not from an Egyptian priest but in fact dated to the 2nd and 3rd centuries AD. In Hermeticism, the ultimate realty is referred to variously as God, the ALL, or THE ONE. God is one and exist apart from the material cosmos.

The **Caduceus** is a symbol of **Hermeticism**:
NOW THIS IS INTERESTING

Look familiar? Nurses? Doctors? EMT?
Medical Field? Healers......
These are the original principals (now looked at as "Laws")

7 Hermetic Principles

1. The Principle of Mentalism- "The all is MIND, The Universe is Mental."
2. The Principle of Vibration- "Nothing rest, everything moves, everything vibrates."
3. The Principle of Correspondence- "As above, so below, as below, so above. As within, so without, as without so within."
4. The Principle of Polarity- "Everything is Dual and has poles or opposites, opposites are identical in nature, but different in degree."
5. The Principle of Rhythm- "Everything flows, out and in, everything has its tides, all things rise and fall, the pendulum-swing."
6. The Principle of Cause and Effect- "Every cause has its effect, every effect has its cause, everything happens according to law."
7. The Principle of Gender- "Gender is in everything, everything has its masculine and feminine principles."

Now, this is amazing stuff. Isaac Newton placed great faith in these concepts. He wrote about the Corpus Hermeticism often and wrote that his writing were transmitted from ancient times in which secrets of the start and forces of nature were revealed. This religion is parallel with early Christianity. I thought it was very interesting to see how our Christian beliefs systems have took some twist and turns over the years.

As above, so below is the Principle of Correspondence- Which means exactly what our trees can teach us.... As above, so below. That which is above corresponds to that which is below to accomplish the miracle of ONENESS. Whatever happens on any level of reality (physical, emotional, mental) happens also on every other level. Does this get you thinking? Make sense? Yes it does but what about all that you have been taught up to this point? Is your programming taking over in your thought process yet? I know for me, this knowledge almost feels like I've hit GOLD. Who would not want to know or understand these principles and apply it to your life?

Failure is NOT Reality
There is no such thing as failure, feedback only

As I mentioned above, decisions are a key aspect of moving in any direction in life. We all have been in that position that there was a vital decision that needed to be made and it was on us to do it. Whatever decision you made makes no difference, whatever outcome you had makes no difference. What does make the difference is the fact that you did make that decision. The most successful people in our life time did not get successful from not making decisions. Move fear aside, make a decision then see your changes unfold in front of you. No more needs to be said.

There Are Spiritual Forces Within Yourself
The KUNDALINI awakening-

We are everything and everything us. There is no separation between you and me and me and you.

The beam of light from top to bottom and bottom to top-
*The **portal** into super-**consciousness***
Have you ever heard of this? Do you study the Bible?
Other Religions?

In America we call the knowledge of the kundalini the "**Holy Ghost**", and it is manifested as tongues of flames over the heads of the apostils during the Pentecost reunion. Moses saw if in the form of the burning bush. During the exodus the Israelites lost their faith and were smitten by fiery serpent so God told Moses "make thee a **serpent and put it upon a pole**, and it shall come to pass, that everyone that is bitten when he looked upon it shall live. And Moses made a serpent of brass and put it on a pole and it came to pass that if a fiery serpent had bitten any man, when he held the serpent of brass he lived." The Bible is FULL OF PARABLES. These stories are significant in the truth of life. Not only that The

113

Koran refers to a similar story, The Toa does, Buddha spoke of it as well and other cultures such as The Greeks and The Egyptians did as well. Any link between the symbol of **Hermeticism** and the description that the Bible uses about Moses putting a serpent on the pole? It only gets more interesting from there. It is not only in the Bible but in so many other religions as well.

In the **Old Testament** this suggest a kundalini awakening "and Moses lift up the serpent in the wilderness even as the son of man be lifted up, that whosoever believeth in him should not perish but have eternal life." **Jesus** says "The **Holy spirit** is my mother, the **Kingdom of God is with in you**." Luke 17:12-----Look at the Hermetic Principles again.

Buddhist- Spoke of the "middle path" to achieve nirvana. He was actually describing the central channel (what the Bible refers to as a pole) through which the Kundalini ascends. This type of link goes on and on in other Religions as well.

This knowledge of the Kundalini awakening is from an ancient knowledge that was once sacred. The **serpent represents the journey of the mind** to matter to the cosmos. Adam and Eve was given knowledge and knowledge was once seen as sinful. The serpent is in all these other religions as well. They all are representing the same thing. One on each side going up our spine, triggering our pineal gland and our brain arc energies, causing it to go up through our entire bodies breaking through the top of our head.

The number 7 is spiritual perfection- In
so many Religions of our world

- 7 chakras
- 7 Hermetic principles
- 7 spikes on statue of liberty
- 7 days, 7 nights
- 7 seals of the bible
- 7 stars on Christ hands
- 7 angles, 7 trumpets
- 7 Heavens

On and on and on……

So what is Kundalini exactly? It is an energy that is creative infinite wisdom that lives inside everyone. Usually is represented as a snake coiled three times and a half around. Kundalini lies dormant at the base of the spine. Not one regular MD will ever be able to X-ray or find physical evidence of this Kundalini. It's not physical- it's spiritual.

This is not another form of religion I am telling you about, it is a part of so many religions and I am simply telling you the facts about this knowledge. Jesus knew about it, Buddha knew about it and there are so many people alive today that understand it and study it in detail. You will not know this unless you do your own research in learning these facts. It is not taught in school anywhere. These facts use to be sacred and people that knew this information in the past were even killed for knowing this truth.

<u>The Gift of Speaking It</u>
A spiritual gift we have
REMEMBER Abracadabra!
Abracadabra by itself means "What you say
becomes" or "I will create as I speak"

Our words are a gift we have to share with the universe. Our words can be used to bless our future or curse our future. When you say I am_____ then that comes to reality. The self-talk you tell yourself is like magic. What you say is. AND not only that, when you tell others something like "I can see_____ for you" then that plants a seed that is like magic that comes into their life. When you make a decision to go into a certain direction, even if the physical aspect of it has not manifested yet, speak about it. Tell others your goals and when you do that things to shift in your paradigm. You have a gift in speaking your future and speaking others as well. Simply put- our words are like saying abracadabra!

Food For The Soul
"My soul needs the Way, the Truth and the life"- John 14:6
"Gracious words are like honey, sweet to the soul
and healthy for the body." Proverbs 16:24

All of this knowledge I am shining a light on is basically food for your soul. Food for our bodies are not fulfilling like food for the soul is. What is food for the soul? Conversation. Have this conversation with yourself. Self-talk is magic and our words are a gift from God, from the higher force in this universe. In this world full of JUNK for the soul with entertainment television hypnotic states, all the horrible news broadcast on a daily bases, and these purposeless events that many hold so high in their life are really NOT health food for the SOUL. What is food for the soul is having knowledge because knowledge is power, use it to grow in wellbeing.

Declutter Your Energy Field
Everything is vibrating
Atoms have empty space

Because we all know by now that it is scientifically proven we all have a energy field we now need to understand that it can become cluttered up. This field of ours can be measured and is a science. The way you feel is a representation of your energy field. Are you feeling low, tired, foggy minded, overwhelmed, living with no passion and have negative thoughts? Then ask yourself what things do you need to let go? What is it that you have too much of in your life? To be at a high frequency state of vibration and attract into our life what we desire we must have balance.

Being in balance with emotions is the first way to de-clutter your energy field. Eat the correct foods for your body. Get in touch with how you feel when you eat this and when you eat that. The truth is not one of us balances our fields the same way or are able to eat the same things to have balance. While I may eat a banana to have balance you may need a cup of yogurt or a hamburger. We cannot hold onto our truths about what we believe is whole foods because the truth is that we are all made up differently.

Too much love and joy makes you out of balance too. You have to rest just as much as you feel that joy. Sleeping or meditation, same benefit. This is so important to maintain your balanced vibration. As you are able to become conscious about how you feel then you will able to control this energy field you have as well. Know that when you wake up every day your energy is cleared.

The first thing in the morning wake up and be thankful for something. Latch on to a thought of the day and share it with others. By being grateful for being in the now, it speeds up your momentum towards what it is in your life that you are desiring. Tune yourself to love and be grateful for you sheets on your bed when you open your eyes. Make this a habit, be grateful for the t-shirt you are wearing and how soft it is. By doing this you take any resistance away from manifesting desires in your life because your focus is on bringing those emotions in that helps you to be tuned in to love, tapped in to the source that is higher than us, and turned on to being conscious of these emotions. Embrace the contrast that you bring to the world, allow yourself to have conversations about some fascinating facts with others and see how the universe will start to bring into your life what you are thinking about.

Part 4
Happiness, Health & Wealth: What does the bill to yourself say?

What Do You Owe Yourself?
"The punishment of desire is the agony of unfulfillment."- Hermes Trismegistus

When you know your value, you start to love yourself. When you start to love yourself you are able to move forward from any circumstance or mistakes you've made in the past. You accept yourself, you accept that it was the past, you accept that you have control of your future and you move in a more healthy direction in life. What happened in you past is something you have NO control over anymore. There is only wasted energy when you look back and when you have negative self-talk inside. Yes, it is an easy thing to say, love yourself but really hard to fathom doing at times in our life. You may look in the mirror cursing your own future by telling yourself what an awful person you are. The truth is every single time you do that, you make that happen in your life. Once you gain a deep understanding of how this works, you will know to instead bless your own future with your self-talk.

Beside my mirror in my bathroom I have placed a chalkboard that says "I am_____" and every single day of my life when I wake up and get ready for my day I look at it. I look at myself and say I am going to achieve great things....and then I say I am going to be an inspiration to others. I go on and on with my positive self-talk. At first it took me a while to believe some of what I was telling myself but as I did it daily for months, I started to believe it. When I started to believe it is when my world drastically shifted. I did the work, I studied about all these principles in life and I dug for information to help myself understand how to love myself more. It takes doing that to really gain insight to some of the greatest knowledge in our universe.

All of life contains in it an energy much greater than itself, an energy that vibrates at a frequency unseen with the naked eye. Our universe is full of life even though some planets appear as if they are dead to us, there are an abundance of other galaxies out there and I know 110% we are not the only life beaming a collected conscious vibration out into the galaxies. Knowing how vase, how large and how grand our universe is YOU MUST learn to accept yourself from this point going forward and let a LOVE energy come through your body so you can illuminate your life! This is what you owe yourself.

Know that **nothing in NEW in life is given birth to without some sort of pain**. The pain from that birth always subsides though and the end result is having a miracle in your hand.

Write yourself a bill- what do you owe yourself?

Is Your World FLAT?

"When Columbus lived, people thought that the earth was flat. They believed the Atlantic Ocean to be filled with monsters large

enough to devour their ships, and with fearful waterfalls over which
their frail vessels would plunge to destruction. Columbus had
to fight these foolish beliefs in order to get men to sail with him.
He felt sure the earth was round." Emma Miler Bolenius, 1919

"He who grasp the truth of the mental nature of the universe is
well advanced on the path to mastery." -Hermes Trismegistus

**Your world, your truths, your beliefs, your reality and
your paradigm** is what you live your life by. Do you **believe** that
if you step out of your comfort zone that **you will fall**? I am here
to tell you that without any doubts that just a false primes that you
are telling yourself. YOUR WORLD IS NOT FLAT. By saying this
I mean it in an abstract way, if you step outside from what you
know and start to gain a broader knowledge of life you will not
fall. You know that there is no such thing as failure that it is only
the universe telling you to go in another direction. You gain insight
into stepping out into the unknown. You realize that it is ONLY
when you START to do that when you WILL FLY instead of falling.
No concretely, not literally fly so do not think I am telling you we
can fly because we cannot without an airplane but we can fly in
an abstract way with living out our life to our full potentials. We
start becoming our higher self, we step outside of our small ways
of thinking, our universe expands and we realize that there is no
falling off into a deep abyss of monsters that will eat us. The higher
power in our life will NEVER allow that to happen once you fully
understand these concepts.

Have you ever thought of this before? Is your world a flat
world? Are you letting fear control your explorations into the
unknown? Are you fearful of coming out of your comfort zone?
Really start to look at yourself and ask yourself this. In the Bible
1 Corinthians 6:19 "Don't you realize that your body is the temple
of the Holy Spirit, who lives in you and was given to you by God?
You do not belong to yourself." And being that God is within us
we know when we have faith in God or that higher power that we
will never fail. "For I, the Lord your God will hold your right hand.
Saying to you, fear not, I will help you" Isaiah 41:13

121

"To hold, you must first open your hand. Let go" **Lao Tzu** said this meaning let go and then you will gain what it is you desire. Understandingly this concept is so simple to grasp once you have the insight and understanding but until you do, until you do the work, until you become aware of this your world will still be perceived as being a flat world.

Stepping Off The Cliff And Flying
"Your wings already exist, all you have to do is fly" unknown

Are you comfortable? Well then get up and do something! Line up with the energy for whatever it takes for you to just do whatever it is you want to do that may not feel so comfortable about it. Push yourself little by little to step out into the unknown. As you step out into this unknown territory you will start to become in touch with how you feel when you get into that zone that is not completely comfortable. This is what life was meant to be like. I am not saying it's not ok to be comfortable because it totally is, I am saying it's not ok to be comfortable completely all the time. This goes back to the knowing that we need balance in our life.

So, when you step off that cliff of that comfort feathered nest that you're in at the moment you will fly. This is a Law of The Universe and its KNOWLEDGE OF OUR ABILITY TO APPLY THIS LAW as well. The knowledge of this makes us secure and confident no matter what. It's the faith aspect, it's the knowing like you know like you know, it's the allowing your desire to manifest. When you find yourself at the edge of your comfort zone, take a deep breath and jump! Do not do this having blind faith unless you know that you are having blind faith. You must have faith that is visionary and able to see what will come.

Go to the very edge of your comfort zone, if you do not know where the edge is, then start to listen to your feelings. Our feelings are what guide us in life. When you want something and feel uncomfortable knowing what you have to do to get there, that's the edge I am talking about. What are you intentions? Are your nerves stopping you? This is the exact point that you need to jump!!! DO not wait because you have the ability to talk yourself down, you won't jump if you talk yourself out of it. Just know that there is a world that is round and when you go to explore it you will not fall off the cliff. There are so many times you have aligned yourself up with what you would love to manifest in your life except these old programmed patterns keep coming up in a cycle in our life. What is preventing my desires to manifest in my life? Your beliefs!!! What do you believe? What are you telling yourself? What is your understanding of the power that you have right now to fly when you step off that cliff?

Flying v/s Failure- A State Of Mind

Practice yourself into allowing & having faith & felling yourself into the fullness of who you are- BOOM! Just that simple- I'll say it again- It takes practice to allow a desire & know your desire will be, pay attention to how you feel to be able to step into the unknown so that you can have a better life.

We know that failure is just what we say failure is, it is a state of mind, and it is a belief. As I have discussed before we must have a deep knowing that failure is not really failure. When you fail at something you've told yourself you've really wanted, ask yourself if you ever really wanted that in the first place. You cannot fail at anything that you deeply and truly have love for. Love, this limitless energy that comes from inside us is the bullseye of intention you should be shooting for with that arrow you have launched of desire. Set your intentions straight, get aligned with it. You can fail at what you do not love so you might as well pay attention to what you do love so that you know you will not fail.

- ❖ "Failure is the opportunity to begin again, only this time more wisely." **Henry Ford**
- ❖ "Our greatest glory is not in never failing, but rising every time we fail." –Confucius
- ❖ "The only real failure in life is not to be true to the best one knows."- Buddha
- ❖ "Think like a queen. A queen is not afraid to fail. Failing is another steppingstone to greatness." Oprah Winfrey

❖ "Failure is success if we learn from it." Malcom Forbes

Do you want to know the difference in a master and a beginner? That master has been through failure many more times than that beginner has. – Think about it.

Recognize Fear and Freedom
"The cave you fear to enter holds the treasure you seek." Joseph Campbell

You have the power to do anything you put your mind to. This statement is simple but complex and at times can seem to not quite match up with our belief about where we are now in life as evidence by our own self-talk. Our conscious minds have the power to direct our subconscious minds since our subconscious does not have the ability to reject any information. Our subconscious mind is where our emotional state originate from without knowing. The fact is we are tapping into parts of our mind we are not comfortable with and stepping out into unknown territory when we face the fears we have internalized. Gaining a better understanding of our own self is not the easiest thing to do. It really does take work and it takes studying about it to truly gain a strong grasp on it.

Our subconscious mind must accept what our conscious mind tells it. It cannot tell the difference between what is real or what is imagined. If you can visualize yourself to do something then you already have it. THAT IS THE TRUTH. Now, it's not like you can just visualize it one time and it manifest in your life. You have to visualize this daily. Not only do you have to visualize this you need to feel it in your heart deeply with an emotional state of love. Let your intentions to whatever it is you are desiring in your life come from a place of love and gratitude. When you do this, study it, see it there in your mind and have it there in your heart regularly and daily then you will be able to also hold it in your hand.

Fear boils down to self-image. Are you the kitten or are you the lion? What is it that you tell yourself about yourself? This knowledge is so powerful. You have to know that YOU are responsible for telling yourself what it is that YOU tell yourself.

AND= what you tell yourself is YOUR TRUTH!!!! Why would you curse yourself? Learn to love yourself so you quit cursing yourself. I don't mean saying dirty words to yourself I mean cursing yourself by claiming ANYTHING that is negative self-talk. Once you are able to recognize this and recognize where your fear is branching from then are will recognize a freedom from your fear!!! It is just that simple. Go in that CAVE and GET YOUR TREASURE!!!

The Universe Is Always Expanding

*"Our universe contains at least **2 trillion galaxies**,*
ten times more than previously thought."- Christopher
Conselice, international lead astronomer- 2017
We live in one of those- the Milky Way galaxy

Facts are the facts, our univerese is expanding at a very fast rate. There are atleast 2 TRILLION galaxies out there and we live in one of them. Astronomers are all beginning to agree that the possibility that life exsist outside of our ONE LITTLE galaxy is pretty promising. I would say knowing these facts that I would agree. Then there is the question of Religion. Knowing this fact, being taught in such ways that debunk any other life than ours, it could cause so many to question every single thing in life they know. Those people that say they are with one religios group or another an do not actually study the source of knowledge in depth that their religion comes from may have issues with this. The truth is God is everywhere even if that is in another galaxy. He created the heavens and he created the Earth. This does not mean he only created Earth. God, the source of the higher power in our life, the energy of empty space in our atoms, the vibration of energy we let out into the universe is everywhere! We have placed GOD in a box in all religions.

I know this is a controversial subjects and wars have went on over and over and over again during years of religion riots and wars. The truth is Jesus was a teacher, not a God but he had knowledge of how our bodies are connected to God. This pertains to other teachers that walked the earth in other religions as well. Gods and Godesses had knowledge that other human beings did not have so they were able to have wisdom about the kundalini when others did not. It's not an idea that lead me to this statement. Jesus knew that we had God in us and even refreces that in the Bible.

This may sound fictitious but it is true- WE LITERALLY ARE MADE OF STARDUST. There is solid science to back this up. Almost every single element on the Earth was formed at the heart of a star. The same EXACT reactions that happen our in space, out in our universe happens INSIDE US!!!! The stars light up because of energy released by nuclear fusion reactions at their cores. There reactions which created chemical elements like carbon or iron. They are the building blocks to everything around us. We light up from these nuclear reactions inside us as well. We are beaming with vibrations that we put out into the atmosphere. We have a forever expanding universe inside of us, beam me up to my highest vibration possible.

Communication with Vibrations and Frequencies of Thoughts

I am not trying to prove anything to anybody I am just trying to live happily ever after-
You are the vibrational translator of your life experience-

Every single cell in our bodies are inundated in an external and an internal environment of unseen magnetic forces that are on a constant fluctuation. Our bodies communicate in a non-verbal and verbal way with each other. The human body has undeniable resources within it for detecting its external environment. Do you agree? Our sense organs are a given and they can distinguish temperature shifts, select ranges of lighting through sight, sound waves that range from low to high, touch on many levels and smell of a numerous amounts.

This non-verbal communication we share among each other is more than just distinguishing the fluctuation of the pupils of the eye or some overt facial expressions or the tone of a voice or any gestures made at all. Evidence studied intensely in our science world supports the fact that an indirect yet significant electromagnetic or energetic communication system operates just below our conscious level of wakefulness.

Have you ever been in an elevator with a group of people not saying a word but are able to look across to the person next to you and sense their emotional state of being? This ability that we have is an important element in allowing us to connect or communicate with them efficiently. As you begin to have a conversation with another person notice how the flow of your conversation is going. When you get into a deep conversation with a person we start to synchronize our movements and postures, vocal pitches, how loud our voices gets, length of pauses between responses and now as science proves this, important aspects of their physiology also can become linked and synchronized. What does this mean exactly? It means that our **NERVOUS SYSTEM** acts like an **ATENA** which is tuned to and responds to magnetic fields produced by the hearts of other individuals. This type of communication is called "energetic communication." This type of communication is believed to be the ability that amplifies our awareness and facilitates important features of true empathy and sensitivity to others. This communication is reported to be an enhanced and deepened communication skill we have as humans.

The way we communicate with our vibrations, our electromagnetic filed is a key aspect into heightened communication. Our hearts is the most powerful source of this energy and the vibration that we have is largely responsible from our heart. It is proven that our electromagnetic filed around us is produced 100 times more from our hearts than from our brains. The research done by a group called HeartMath is amazing. They even proved that our hearts become synchronized with our animal's hearts. This claim can be measured and logged and is a part of an intense research done on this communication.

Our thoughts from our brain control our emotions and our emotions control our nervous system responses and our nervous system responses control our heartbeats. All of the research is very detailed on this subject and most people are oblivious to this at all. This is something that our news channels should be talking about and instead of the negativity in our world. A deep explanation of this is not needed when looking at the reports from the EEG and EKG reports from a various group of people and animals. The truth is we communicate and call into our life situations, circumstances and people that match our vibrations.

Do you get it? Our thoughts control emotions, emotions control our heart, our heart controls our vibration, and our vibration controls our outcome- simply put- proven by science.

What Do You Tell Yourself?

Are you wobble free?
You WILL NOT GET IT- until you GIVE it-
Attitude is EVERYTHING

Our economy today forces us all to work for survival. We trade time for money. Though money should not be the reason we work and many of us fall into this category. Do you tell yourself you work for money? I quit telling myself that once I learn this simple amazing truth. Work is only to serve others and to serve others will produce emotions inside that will align you with what your destiny is. Because you start to look at what you do as just a form of service instead of the money making aspect of a job it changes your attitude towards getting up and clocking in. Not only that, you start to realize that trading your time for money is not the only thing you have the capability of to produce money inflow into your life. Some of the richest people in our world today do not clock in for their inflow of money. What have they been telling their self? What are they doing that you are not doing? These are the questions I started to ask myself along with all the other questions I have going on in my brain.

We earn money by trading our time for money, by investing in money to earn money and the more important way by having multiple sources of income. Bob Proctor teaches courses on earning money while you sleep by having MSIs and highlights that only 1% of our population does this. I have studied his teachings along with some other super humans in our world. Realizing that trading my time for money was not what I wanted to do ever again in my life, I started digging for answers on how to not do that. By studying so many different outlets for this subject I was lead on a spiritual path into some unknown truthful knowledge I was unaware of. The key lessons I have come to understand is that having a state of balance in our life is vital to maintain wellbeing and my wellbeing was WAY more valuable than any amounts of materialistic things or money could bring me.

By learning that my service to others was important to come from my heart I started shifting my world by my thoughts. Often I have people asking me why I am so happy, mainly it is because I understand I am in control of my own happiness and give nobody else control of that aspect. I also understand that my emotions control my vibration it is what my vibration is speaking into the universe that brings me abundance in life. It is not in a form of money at all. I am sure you can ask anyone that is rich and unhappy if they are whole just because of their wealth and they would tell you no. A new car cannot bring you balance in life, a nice new home does not bring balance. You see, I've figured out that you have to have **balance FIRST** in order to get these other things in your life. Balance in life means you are happy with YOUR NOW, you are happy with your current situation. When you are able to get to the balanced point in your life then it attracts what is in alignment with your vibration which is ONLY MORE POSITIVE THINGS!

It may be hard to understand this at first but as soon as you do, you've got it for life. When you can start telling yourself that you care about how you feel, your attitude changes. You quit looking at the service that you are providing as your only source of income because it is a law of the universe. If you want more than just the money you are making at your job and you think about *other* ways to make money you WILL MAKE money from other sources. Why did I not apply this to my life before now? It is only because it took me a while to figure this out but once I really studied it and worked hard to understand it, I got it.

Disease and Being At Ease
Is it possible to think beyond what is?
Your sickness or wellbeing- which do you focus on more?

Being at ease with yourself, your past, your present, your body, your mistakes, your failures and all other aspects that make you who you are is so vital to being at ease in life. Sounds easy to do I know but most of us are not at ease. By being at dis-ease in our life we bring disease to our life. Our vibrational alignment gets all out of control and we actually bring on sickness into manifestation. The more negative thoughts you tell yourself the more your body absorbs that frequency vibration and brings more of that onto us. Negative brings more negative. So, this is the lesson here. Focus your thoughts on wellbeing instead.

When you get sick instead of focusing on that sickness focus on everything about who you are that you are grateful for and that you are able to do. I can understand this being a controversial subject here but the truth is we can bring on sickness in our life just by being in a negative state of mind. If you have sickness in your body at this time focus on the feeling of how you would feel being in a state of ease, a state of wellbeing. Appreciate life and what you have to give to others, how you can give service to another human being. What you focus about, you bring about.

Our Bodies Are Made of Flesh
We are deeper than skin-
STARDUST

"Christ has no body now, but yours......... No hands.....No feet.....on earth....but yours. Yours are the eyes through which Christ looks compassion into the World. Yours are the feet with which Christ walks to do good. Yours are the hand with which Christ blessed the world." – Saint Teresa of Avila- This quotes expresses the knowledge Saint Teresa had that Christ is in us, God is in us and we are more than just a body. God, the higher power of our universe is in our universe and did not only create Earth but he created the heavens as well. He created those trillions of other galaxies floating in a time space reality of their own. God created the universe inside and outside of us. All of humanity has a universal consciousness we must become aware of, this knowledge I am about to share should open up some questions to ask yourself.

You are STARDUST. Your entire physiological structure is composed of the fragments of stars that exploded billions of years before you were even perceived to be given the breath of life. Your entire body structure is made up of cosmic fragments of immeasurable proportion. Evolutionary mindset shifts, awaken your souls to have a deeper knowledge— "There is no fact in science that is more awe-inspiring and deeply meaningful than that we are made of stardust, the remnants of exploded stars billions of years ago that through the process of evolution have turned into conscious creatures into humans.: Michael Shermer

"The most astounding fact is the knowledge that
the atoms that comprise life on Earth,
the atoms that make up the human body,
are traceable to the crucibles ***that cooked light elements
into heavy elements*** in their core under
extreme temperatures and pressures.

These stars, ***the high mass ones among
them***, went unstable in their later years.
They collapsed and then exploded,
Scattering their enriched guts across the galaxy.
***Guts made of carbon, nitrogen, oxygen and all
the fundamental ingredients of life itself.***"
Neil DeGrasse Tyson

This speech hits home with me in an enormous way. The facts are the facts and we as a collective consciousness need to wake up as we start to have a deep understanding of this. As Michael Brant Shermer, **a historian of science, founder of Skeptics Society** says "We are, in fact, made FROM THE STARS. Our ATOMS were forged in the interior of ancient stars that ended their lives in spectacular paroxysms of supernova explosions that dispersed those atoms into space, where they coalesced into new solar systems with planets, life, and sentient beings capable of such SUBLIME KNOWLEDGE and moral wisdom." Our bodies are flesh and blood and made of stardust. How does this knowledge make you feel? Can you feel your spirit rising in the knowing that we are not just matter but as a matter of fact we have the universe inside of us?

Write Your Price Tag, Your Value, Your Belief

Un-do unwanted programming
Reprogram your life
Reprogram your mind
Rejuvenate your consciousness
We truly are ONE as a WHOLE
Our UNIVERSE IS MENTAL

Knowing that our bodies are more than the eye is able to comprehend we must raise our standard of how we are placing a value on ourselves. I am not sure who programmed you or who for that matter exactly programed me but I can say it was not one person. It was all of the collected experiences I held in my mind's eye from a baby and on. It was those old school television shows, the routine of school, the people that I grew up around and every single person that walked into and OUT of my life. It was the environment, the swing that hung from the tree branch that I lived my afternoons on, it was the people in the crowd while I sang in choir in church as a girl, it was my science teacher in 6th grade Mr. Dixon and my art teacher in high school Mr. Arewood. I am only trying to make a point in giving a simple understanding of universal consciousness. Every one of us plays a role in all the individuals that cross our paths at any given moment even if it is one direct moment. Becoming aware of this we as a whole will learn that our beliefs must match balance needed on Earth. **Our Earth is mental, the universe is mental.**

What does this mean? The universe is mental? It is the first Hermetic Principle and for some, difficult to understand. Once we all begin to understand this principle is when we WILL see dramatic shifts in our Earth. Our Earth is balanced as it needs to be and there is only EXPANSION that is to be gained. The reason why I do not say our Earth is in need of change is because I choose to focus on WELBEING instead of the sickness. Choose to focus on the wellbeing of Earth- and what we focus about, we bring about. A well balanced Earth. The yin and the yang – the earth as a whole in perfect balance with the ebb and flow of life. Everything vibrates and there is no pretending when saying that as science has proven this.

Be mindful of your self-talk, it is in conversation with our universe. Knowing this, what is your value? Instead of cursing your future, bless it with your self-talk. Do you know your own worth? What is your value? This 50,000 year old book about the Hermetic Principles was deeply understood by the Egyptians and as we begin to have an understanding that this is the truth our universe will shift in consciousness. Our thoughts create our world. With your thoughts write your price tag!

Something For Nothing
The sweetness of doing nothing- focus.

Do you really want something? Combining your understanding of the laws of the universe, your own nature of being, of your spiritual being is what will keep your going regardless of anything in your past or any bumps in the road. There is nothing in your way that can ever stop you from going once you grasp this knowledge. You will keep looking forward and place value on your feelings more. You have control of how you feel. Inspired action comes from a powerful good feeling vibration and an inspiration comes it only adds momentum or speed to something. When the energy inside is moving in a flow so doing something by doing nothing is actually focusing or "getting in the ZONE." IT means that that you are doing something that is alignment of who you really are so it feels as if you really are not doing anything because it flows so freely. When your vibration is low you just want to do nothing and you think it's actually a good place to be in. But thinking about this concretely is not ever resignation parallel with the laws of our universe. Some of us may have a **misunderstanding** of the law of vibration or the law of attraction. It does not mean you can just WISH something BOOM- into existence. You must study and align yourself with it. So getting something for nothing really means focusing on your desire and really getting into a free flowing vibration that will allow it to manifest in your life.

Treat Yourself and Others How YOU Want TO Be Treated
Say to yourself- "Something good is going to happen to me today"
Hold that belief.

As you begin to understand how to line up with your inner self and know that you are the controller of your emotions you have a clearer vision of how you want to be treated. Clarity is key in knowing how to treat yourself and how to treat others. Treat yourself though, it is a part of the balancing act in wellbeing. We must learn to treat ourselves. Feeling good is an addiction, I mean feeling good at the natural state with no outer synthetic ways to feel better. Where our emotions come from are our own thoughts. It is our emotions that drive our life. God will not move through your body to the fullest of alignment unless you learn to love who you are. Treat yourself, love yourself.

When I find myself having any negative thoughts come to me, I go very general in my conscious thoughts. For example, when I feel annoyed by anything instead I can recognize it and say "love, love, love, love, love, love, love, love" over and over again to myself until I start feeling good again. Sounds a little silly doesn't it? It is really a good practice to have though. Another thing I have learned to do is when I feel anxious for whatever reason I start to use Abraham Hicks focus wheel tool to put me back into the vibration of love for myself. When you learn to love who you are inside and out then you can love others to that same level. You will learn to not pass any judgements but know as you learn to do this that others in your life will not understand this unless they are also in their alignment as well. You will find yourself not being able to tolerate negative talk at all because you know you would rather feel good than to get that negative energy momentum going.

How Do You Relate To Others?
Split energy- this or that

Doubt makes more doubt. When you know something you do not need anyone else to know it, all you need to do is know that you know. Never proceed with a conversation that gets off on the wrong foot. A teacher is only as effective as his skill to stand where his student is, to have empathy. The most important thing to do in any form of communication is to stay lined up with who you are. Do not force others to come over to your side in their own view of what it is they are perceiving. Everyone has their own eyes and most of the time when conflict arises in your life its perception that is the cause.

My perception of this reality and yours are totally different. We all have our own opinions that move our emotions which cause our actions. For example have you ever had a friend that breaks up with their significant other and then that same day makes up with them? Your friend has talked all this negative and unjust treatment that they have been getting from their significant other. You may start to see it their way if this goes on long enough. Then, they get back together that night and ask you to come eat dinner with them. The thing is, you've been set up to stay in a certain vibration about their relationship because it is what has been reflected on to you. You have been invited vibrational to have that perception. The thing is when that friend gets back with them they have not offered any positive vibrations about that relationship back to you. It is law of attraction at its best. If you want a person to perceive anything you have to offer the vibration and it comes back to you by this law. It relates to the Hermetic principle of rhythm. When you extend kindness to another person with no terms of receiving a reward to this is the way to directly connected to the source of higher power. When others are treating you a certain way it is ONLY a reflection of what you have offered them.

When you want to connect or relate with others on a higher level of vibration find ONE thing about those people that is positive. Instead of focusing on how much you are in disconnect with them focus about one thing that you do connect with them about. This is how you will change your relationship with a large group of people. It is not only for a large group of people but this applies to any relationship in your life. If you are married and having a rough time at the moment, it is because you are only focusing on the negative aspects of that person instead of focusing on the positive contributions. This is the law of attraction and in the law of attraction there is a principle applied called the principle of rhythm. This is one of the seven hermetic principles and this knowledge is golden once you start applying it to your life.

Hermetic Principle of Rhythm:
Everything flows, out and in, everything has its tides, all things rise and fall, the pendulum sing manifest in everything, **the measure of the swing to the right is the measure of the swing to the left**, rhythm compensates.

This principle is a part of Hermeticism. I've spoken of it before but did not go into great detail about the history. Basically these principles came from a book that was found and translated that Egyptian and Greek people followed as wisdom about our universe. Hermes Trismegistus was a philosopher and these principles pulled for the original script of that book are pre-dated back to humanity's "sacred scriptures" and are a part of the source of our world's original sacred knowledge. Hermes is said to be a combination of the Greek "god" Hermes and the Egyptian "god" Thoth. So basically these two "Gods" were worshiped as one. The word "God" references to someone who has been Enlightened and has sacred knowledge, a messenger from God, the higher power of the universe. Just FYI.

Are You Lucky? Say It! and Then It Is
*There is **science** behind being lucky and unlucky- proved*

This concept is **PROVEN to be a FACT**. Basically if you tell yourself you are lucky then you are. If you tell yourself you are unlucky then you are. Why though? Proven fact by multiple studies done on this is the fact that the people who self-identify with being lucky are open for good circumstances in their life verses those who self-identify with being unlucky. There is a science behind luck and **Richard Wiseman** studied this over a period of ten years with multiple experiments.

What is boils down to in a few key concepts are that lucky people are:

- Experienced at creating and noticing those chance opportunities
- Make lucky decisions by pay attention to their intuition
- Generate self-fulfilling prophesies through positive expectations
- Adopt a bounce back attitude that transforms bad luck into good luck

This is only saying in another way that universal laws are put into use when being a lucky person. You are what you say you are. It's what I am trying to show you. Those of you reading this that can say that you are one of those "unlucky" people then you always will be because you get back what you focus on with your heart, mind and spirit.

Principles of Science and the Laws of The Universe

Seven Principles of Science
Law of individuality
Principle of Exchange
Law of Progressive Change
Law of comparison
Law of analysis
Law of probability
Law of circumstantial facts
&
Spirituality- the unseen force of nature

There is no denying that since human beings are always needing to see proof that something exist then scientific excitements are created to do that. Using the universe principles and laws I have discussed in this book so far are a key concept in creating change and manifesting desires in your life. To maintain

137

balance is not hard once it has been practiced. Having not only wealth in your life but having happiness and having your health will give you an overall state of living as a well-being human being and having wellbeing. By using our science principles we can prove that our universe gives us back what we are aligned to vibrational. Watch your thoughts because our universe hears them. Write your value. How much are you worth?

Part 5
The Success Principle, Going the Extra Mile: Are you at a turning point?

Quality, Quantity, Mental Attitude

"Your mental attitude is something you can control outright and you must use self-discipline until you create a positive mental attitude- your mental attitude attracts to you everything that makes you what you are." Napoleon Hill

A positive mental attitude can clear away any obstacles you may face in life. To keep our minds positive use these key concepts:

> Learn to be flexible
> Studying these concepts
> Choose your battles
> Laugh often
> Have Gratitude for the contrast in your life
> Know that you can do it
> Learn to have a habit that helps you remember where you want to be (goal card)
> Recognize every circumstance as growth- good or bad, no failure
> Learn something new every day- good or bad
> Work on yourself and be more open minded

➤ Express gratitude that you have the knowledge of self-control
  ➤ Comment on good qualities of those around you daily
    ➤ Accept all criticism of yourself to grow from
    ➤ Do not accept anything that you do not want
  ➤ Remember there are two circumstances that cause worry-
      ➤ Keep your mind engaged in your desires
      in life instead of what you do not want
        ➤ Do not feel sorry for yourself
  ➤ Choose someone to look up to and reflect their actions
      ➤ Develop your tone of voice that is inviting
      ➤ Place your chalk board quote by a mirror
      that you can see "I am_____"
    ➤ Know if you can hold the idea in your mind, have
    it in your heart then you will see it in your hands

Napoleon Hill calls the "**QQMA formula**" which means "the quality of service or product you provide and the quantity of that which you provide and the mental attitude in which you provide it determines how successful you become." He was beyond his time born in 1883 but wrote some amazing literature to help others along the way. His lessons are still held of great value in today's self-help community of writers. Bob Proctor gives his success to Napoleon Hill's book called "think and grow rich."

What Do You Accept?

Only accept positive self-talk. As you read through this book there are some major key points I hit on that will help anyone move forward in life. Looking at your life through a different perception of vision in a higher state of being is only going to provide your life with the abundance you need to carry on during your life on Earth.

Want A Better Circumstance?
Get into the feeling of wonder, surprise, enthusiasm, feeling of being interested, eagerness, satisfaction, appreciation and love- consistently and in the now.

We should all be in a state of continuous expansion when we are in alignment with our true self. Have you ever thought about how time seems to go much faster as you get older? The thing is yes, I've heard this from multiple people, the years get shorter and the days get shorter. The fact of the matter is this is all about perception. Time is perceptual. To have expansion we must be in the receptive mode. There is give and take in life but the balance of give it to take, is to receive. You have the ability to perceive much more in the receptive mode so your life becomes really really full of so much, of so many things to do. So really, all that is happening is the fact that you have so much to do in your days that time seems to pass by faster. Does that make sense? Every once measures time differently.

It is to the degree that you are or are not connected to God or the source of higher power that represents your true perspective of time. The thing is time…and dollars too…should be taken out of the equation all together. Who you are and what you know is unique to you so at this moment you've had an expanded moment in the learning of these different concepts. We should be focusing on expansion in our life instead of time or money. Quit focusing on time so much and then you are able to get into the flow of the high flowing energy to do so. This lesson pertains to all of us.

As we expand we should be gathering knowledge that helps us plug into that which is a higher power here on earth, a higher source of energy that raises our vibrations that will bring you to your true sense of self. Once we get there it is a Law of the Universe that we expand, our world expands, our universe expands and we have the outcome of a better circumstance. The signal that you start to emit is a signal of expansion because that is what you are focused on.

Know that every single subject you focus on has contrast in it. Imagine a desire like a stick with two ends. On one end is that which you desire and that which you do not desire. A larger part of us tend to lean into the direction of that end on the stick that is the desire end, that which you desire end. It is nice to know you are getting constant steady feedback. What you are looking for is compatibility with the vibration of that higher perspective. The reason why this matters is you keep expanding to that higher perspective. In our body we sit having different experiences, knowing our desires and knowing what we do not want. Every time you are going through an experiences, you are launching your rockets of desires and when this happens you are expanding. This vibrational reality exist. These vibrations you put out as signals come from your thoughts and emotions. Life cause you to expand and you do not keep up with it you begin to not feel good.

As life causes you to expand and you do not keep up with the expansion, you do not feel so good. In other words, if you have desires that are not met or brought into manifestation you get upset. Correct? You want a new car and you do not see a new car in your life it can cause you to start the doubt. When you start the doubting of it is when that vibrational signal gets sent out into the universe and that is what you get back. To want something and to doubt it, you feel bad. Care about the tuning of you, get yourself into alignment of who you are and quit caring about everyone else perception around you. This is when you are able to send a strong signal out and then it must come. The desire will come in the see it, hear it, taste it, touch it now manifestation of your desire.

You have to adjust your vibration to see the reality of your expansion. It's the same as getting from point A to point B. The small details are unknown but do not turn around when you do not get there as fast as you thought you would, keep going on that path. Embrace the contrast that life has to offer and that you yourself has to offer life. You are the translator of the signal you have let out. You cannot stop wanting things or your expansion. Do not focus on the NOW of which is only the manifestations of your past. It also goes back to the idea of how you gain weight in your physical body. You eat 12 donuts every day for 12 weeks long then you gain a few pounds. That weight gain is because of your past. You did not just gain weight over night! This is also used as an example of how things manifest in your life. What you do now is just that and what you have now is from your past thoughts. Know that these desires will come and get lined up with the feel good of knowing that it will come. Just know you will get there. Everything is all about perception.

Want to be Compensated For Your Services?
The Law of Compensation

This law states there are three things that produce the outcome you have in your career. The need for what you do, your ability to do it and the difficulty there will be in replacing you. Think about this for a little while. You really only need to focus on your ability to do it more than anything out of those three points. Because the need for what you do is already there and your ability to do it measures the difficulty that there is in replacing you. Get better at what you are doing. No competition expect for with yourself.

Bob Proctor talks about three strategies for earning money called" M1, M2 and M3." We must teach our children this concept, this is not taught in school at all. M1 is used by MOST of the population and it does not work as far as compensation goes. "M1 is where you trade your TIME for MONEY." You always run out of time. M2 is only used by a very small percentage of people. This is where people basically make money off of money like interest grown and investments. M3 is used by 1 person out of 100 people of our population and is why we have a TINY super rich population. "M3 is when you have multiple sources of income" Mr. Proctor says. Not multiple jobs, it's having multiple sources of income that will produce your income while you snooze. I just thought this was interesting because I never really thought about it. As I came into this knowledge my brain started launching rockets of desires that will no doubt manifest in my life. Our world is changing because of our technologies. The truth is we have access to the whole world to set up a means of multiple sources of income. We are all capable of doing this then our compensation will defiantly increase.

Excel In Your Line Of Work

Pay attention to how you feel. This is the most important thing to excel in anything. Studies have shown that your attitude, which is connected to your emotions, create outcomes in your everyday life. Your attitude effects so many aspect of your daily life. Get tuned in to your emotional state of being in the higher vibration and get aligned to pure positive energy. Allow yourself to connect to the you of who you really are because we all come from a place of pure love. Ask, allow and trust. Trust the process. Be flexible like water and soft like water.

Contrast and How it Plays Into Success

I have spoken of the contrast that life has to offer in this book and explained that it is what makes life life. Although contrast sometimes gives an unknown outcome, it is what life is all about. The contrast can be unwanted and wanted. It is the thing in our picture of life that makes the picture we hold in of our life pop. Without contrast our experiences would be black and white. That's no fun at all! Why do you think color television exist? We are attracted to having that contrast. We are not robots although we may at times feel as if we live a robotic lifestyle with day to day routines. The truth is embracing the unknown small details of your everyday life is what makes it FUN to be alive. If we knew how each day would go over and over again it would be like we were in some fictional Hollywood movie. That is not the reality!!!! What reality is... is the fact that there is contrast that we put out into the world and contrast that others put out into the world. There is good and bad but either equally as important.

Get into the mindset that everything is happening around you due to the fact that you are the one that created it. Our thoughts are heard by the universe because the universe it mental. It hears the smallest whispers in your head about any random subject you think about. This is so true once you learn how to tune into this attraction law. Stay in the vibration of positive thoughts as much as you can. This takes practice and it takes learning how to go general with your thoughts when you find negativity creeping in.

<u>Be Original</u>

Self-expression is just another creative aspect that human beings have. It plays right there parallel to imagination and art. Our finger prints are all different and our perceptions are all different. My reality is not yours and yours not mine. Once you learn that you are able to control your emotional state by just making a clear decision to feel good then everything else starts to fall into place in your life. Feeling good and caring about how you feel is so important. To be able to feel good we need to let go of the past situations so they do not define us.

Let go of the good and let go of the bad. Look straight ahead in life without looking back to have a clear vision of how you want your future to play out. For example you are the diver of a car staying in your lane and there are other cars coming in the opposite direction in their lane. Your family and friends are your passengers if you turn around to look at them and take your eyes off the road then you may swerve into the other lane and hit another car. Then what? You've crashed and people get hurt. So, this lesson is about focus. Focus on where you are going and know that you do have others along for the ride. What you do effects all those people around you just as much as it impacts you. Cause and effect. It's not rocket science yet we are blinded to this simple lesson at times.

Being original means lining up with who you are inside. It means getting back to the free flowing frequency of a high vibration of love that flows to you, through you, in you and back out of you. Love yourself and know everything will work out perfectly but understand that faith is so important. Hold in your hearts the desires you wish to obtain and imagine them in your hands. Take frequent mental breaks throughout your day to really focus on your goals for the quarter of the year that you've imagined for yourself to achieve. Get conscious with your thought process. Understand that holding on to the past is a main reason you feel depression and living in the future is what brings that anxiety to your life. Instead be in the now and focus on feeling good as much as you allow yourself to.

Imagination To Gain Advancement
"Logic will take you from A to B, IMAGINATION will take you EVERYWHERE." Albert Einstein

Even though Albert Einstein understood the value of imagination, it does not take being a Genius scientist to have this understanding. Having the insight into your own future plays a HUGE role in personal advancement. It has been proven over and over again that if you are able to perceive something then you are able to achieve it. Imagination and intelligence work together in our brains to go beyond where you are into advancement.

Be Self- Reliant
"It's your road and yours alone.
Others may walk it with you, but no one can walk it for you." Rumi

Being self-reliant means that you understand that you are the one in control of your emotions, thoughts, actions and therefore your manifestations. Yes, God is with you along the way as a connection to plug yourself into that is where all of whatever is and whatever will be. You are in control of imagining your future and having faith that it will present itself as reality in your life. Not one person is more special than another person. Some may know how to be self-reliant and if you have not figured that out yet you may have the idea that some just have more luck than you do or some kind whimsical gift. The truth is we all, each and every one of us has this power to unlock our own full potential. Know that the results you see in your life today and only from your thoughts of yesterday. Go beyond that logical mindset and use the imaginative key we have as humans to propel yourself to another dimension.

Master Procrastination
Be decisive- Power

Infinite intelligence, creative imagination, accumulated experience, experiments and research are all it takes to have power in life. Obtaining knowledge from either one of these four sources may be used and turned into power by organizing it into definite plans then conveying those plans by action. If you are able to carry your goals out with persistence and enthusiasm then you have mastered procrastination.

Napoleon Hill said "Do it now!!! Can affect every phase of your life. It can help you do the things you should do but don't feel like doing. It can keep you from procrastinating when an unpleasant duty faces you. But it can also help you do those things that you want to do. It helps you seize those precious moments that, if lost, may never be retrieved." This goes back to the rule I follow that Mel Robbins wrote of book on called the five second rule. Basically you have a task, you don't want to do it but then you count 5, 4, 3, 2, 1 then launch like a rocket to do it. This rule is huge in my daily life, every morning when I wake up after I have had those thoughts of appreciation I count instead of hitting the snooze button. It works and makes you a more productive person.

What is Your Purpose? Your Intent?

Can I grow? Do you always have to have
more? How do you define expansion?
You already are limitless.........

Your circumstances have very little to do with what you have in life. Is this an absurd comment to you? I mean, what you have as far as the materialistic things you have do not define what you have. Does that make sense to you? Take what you have and accept it. Accept yourself. Take your life in your own hands and know that EVERYTHING that crosses your path is a BLESSING. Good or bad, yes....Good or bad. The reason why this is so is because God is perfect. You can say that when you see the ocean, when you get into a non-resistant state and focus on your breathing in front of a magical body of water that God created. It's argumentative when you have some sort of disappointment or failure that you may argue that God is not perfect. Everything comes about from a thought. Every single item, this book you are reading came from a thought from me. The shoes you wearing, the bracelet on your wrist or the hairband you tie your hair back with. These things were only thoughts. This means, there is an unseen world, our thoughts. How do you choose to think? What is your intent in life?

Creative visualization takes practice to master. I created the image of myself holding my book I wrote in my hand, this is how this book came about. During this book I am in school full time and working as an aesthetic nurse injector and working with three plastic surgeons. This book was written in less than 2 months. From January 15- February 27 along with all the other things in my universe. I can honestly say that this book came from a higher source that I was able to be tapped into in order to achieve my goal that I wrote for myself. Success depends on self-motivation which comes from reaching that higher vibration with your thoughts and emotions but also being in alignment with that magnificent force of love, God. This visualization manifested in my own hands but first started as a thought.

99% of who you are you are unable to see and touch, correct? Our souls? Can you see your soul? No, you cannot. Can you see life? Do you only see a body when you think about what life is? What about those bodies that we define as lifeless then? Life doesn't die, it only transforms though. The idea that seeing yourself as love and only having that ALONE to give away will transform your paradigm creating that paradigm shift within you. Let love be you ONLY intent for every single thing you do and watch. Observe this limitless life unfold for you.

Become in Alignment With Others

Everything that happens to you in life contains a lesson. Does not matter what this is, there is a lesson in it. DO not curse the things that come your way, do not blame others because you have control over how you feel. "He hurt my feelings" how? Without your consent he cannot hurt you. Understand that they have their own perception and they are only reflecting their own vibrational state of being. You cannot allow your vibration to become in sync with theirs by giving consent to do so.

We all are different. We all have different fingerings, smells, looks, perceptions and so forth. You are always you and I am always me. When you get into a relationship know that you are still one person. You are not a half person going into a relationship becoming one with another person. The truth is you are a single person with that other person. It doesn't matter if you are married or in a long term relationship, you are still two single people. You are you and the person who is not trying to love but IS LOVE, who lives love and that is being love. God is love correct? Well you have to be love...." Whoever does not love does not know God, because God is love" 1 John 4:8. So it is by knowing that love for yourself and love for others is KEY in being a NO LIMIT person you are able to line up with every single person that is meant to be in your life.

Use Nature to Help With The Force Needed- Mother Nature's Habits

Principles of the universe!!!!
Do you get mango juice from an orange?
Really? Apple juice from a mango?
Use the world around you as lessons, nature
teaches us things beyond the seen.

Mother Nature teaches us many lessons on a daily bases. Some of these lessons are on a larger scale than others but some are just so simple with such strong lessons. Take a mango for example, you cannot get orange juice from this mango right? You say no Eva, that's crazy. Follow me so that it's clear for your understanding about this much needed valuable lesson. You cannot without any doubt squeeze an orange and get apple juice right? Why is that? Because that orange only has orange juice in it!!! Does it matter who squeezes it? NO!!! If your friend squeezes it you will still see orange juice from an orange. Well duh!!

SAME PRINCIPLE WORKS FOR YOU!!! What about when someone places you under pressure? What comes out? What is inside of you? Love? Hate? Anger? Bitterness? Joy? Excitement? You get my point now? You cannot put out into the universe what's not inside of you. So seeing yourself as love is a way to the limitless life wouldn't you say it's important to be full of love? Who puts what gets inside of you inside of you? **YOU DO!!!** Your thoughts DO!!! Enjoy the NOWNESS of your present moment and start living your life from a different perspective. All that is in the world today that you are able to see, taste, touch and feel is only a small fraction of what is important for living in that state of wellbeing in life. The more important faculties are within us, **the unseen** and living in vibrational alignment with the higher source of being. We must all learn to stop reaching outside of ourselves to achieve what we define as success, instead go within and line up with that abundance source of energetic love flow coming to you from a never ending source. Let it flow to you, in you, through you and back out into the universe.

Made in United States
Orlando, FL
09 September 2022

22237835R00096